God's Heart As It Relates To Foreknowledge - Predestination

Written by Bob Warren

Much thanks to the following saints who devoted countless hours to the production of this work:

Trey Alley
Brent Armstrong
Dan Carter
Myra Cleaver
Jhonda Johnston

Copyright © 2012 The Hill Publishing/B.A.S.I.C. Training, Inc.
2nd Edition, December 2013
This material may not be reprinted in any form without permission.
www.lifeonthehill.org

ISBN: 978-1-62727-020-5

All scripture, unless otherwise noted, is from the New American Standard Bible.

Table of Contents

Part One

Chapter One

Part Two

Chapter Two

Part Four

Chapter Six

Chapter Seven

Chapter Eight

Chapter Nine

PART ONE ❧ CHAPTER ONE

PURPOSE

The Necessity Of This Series

The original twelve apostles viewed the Scriptures as God breathed and infallible, and contradiction was in no way classified as vogue. Words were defined in granite and could not, under any circumstance, be redefined. Thus, words retained their meaning, which meant that God's Word, interpreted in context, was the final say.

Times have changed. Times have drastically changed. In the post-modern era of today, systems of thought are upheld, even when Scripture must be bent or compromised in an attempt to validate these systems' ideologies. Biblical terms are redefined, leaving the final say with the writer or teacher, to the ruin of many. If you doubt these statements, go to almost any university in America and ask Who Jesus is and what He made available to man. Ask how man can be saved and what part God plays in salvation. You will hear a plethora of answers that, in many cases, diametrically opposes the teachings of Scripture. Like it or not, we live in this predicament and it should break our hearts. Such falsehoods have painted a picture of God that is not only incorrect, but totally misrepresents His Person. As a result, hoards of believers, yes believers, have given up on pursuing God's true identity and have settled for a God shrouded with compromise and contradiction.

Such falsehoods have painted a picture of God that is not only incorrect, but totally misrepresents His Person.

The Full Counsel

God is truth. His Word is truth, that is every word interpreted in the context in which it is written. As a result, I consider any system of thought, even within Christendom, as accountable to the full counsel of God's Word—every word, phrase, verse, chapter, and book. In other words, if any portion of God's Word refutes any of my beliefs, then those beliefs are incorrect and must be jettisoned.

Nothing Hidden

I owe it to you as a teacher to hide none of what I believe regarding the Creator. Consequently, my heart and soul are not only embedded in the confines of this work, but are laid bare before you as well. My policy is to speak and write what I deem to be truth and trust God with what transpires. This mindset has served me well over the years. Please overlook my weaknesses as a communicator, however, and trust God's Word, interpreted in context, to make this endeavor worth your time. Should I become your enemy by telling you the truth (Galatians 4:16), I would appreciate your telling me why, especially if my words lack sensitivity and compassion. I trust, therefore, that my passion will not be perceived as arrogance, but rather as what it really is—a burden for God's people to properly view the Creator and correctly portray Him to man.

Benefiting All

All people, regardless of their level of maturity, can benefit from this study—even should they disagree with its bottom line. After all, if we are confident in what we believe, we should welcome any argument against what we accept as truth. If not, we have become unteachable, a dangerous condition indeed. Therefore, welcome aboard as we embark on a journey that is second to none, a journey to the core of God's loving, compassionate, and gracious heart.

PART TWO ❧ CHAPTER TWO

INTRODUCTION

Some Highly Debated Topics

PREDESTINATION, ELECTION, FOREKNOWLEDGE, the believer's chosenness, depravity, sovereignty, free will, the security of the believer, limited or unlimited atonement, the hardening of Pharaoh's heart, and an assortment of related subjects are highly divisive and extremely volatile. In fact, they are at the forefront of many debates among believers today. Yet, these subjects are vital issues that must be discussed and clarified because they, as much as any of the doctrines addressed in God's Word, directly affect how God is perceived by man.

The Significant Issue of Life

A correct perception of God, Who is *"eternal,"* is the chief goal of life. For this reason Jesus stated:

> *"And this is eternal life, that they may know thee, the only true*
> *God, and Jesus Christ whom Thou has sent.* (John 17:3)

Jesus was speaking of more than a minimal knowledge of God. He was referring to an intimate knowledge of the Creator, which results from making God your very best Friend.

Paul understood this same truth. A correct, proper, and healthy view of God's heart was his passion throughout his many years of ministry. As a result he wrote:

> *That I may know Him, and the power of His resurrection and the*
> *fellowship of His sufferings...* (Philippians 3:10)

9

God is love (1John 4:8, 16). A believer must know the God of love if his/her faith is to work *"by love"* (Galatians 5:6)—love being the motivation that sustains the believer over time. The resource that reveals His heart is His Word (made revelation through the Person of the Holy Spirit), which cannot be studied passively and out of context but must be examined diligently and in context, making sure that no conclusion is contradictory to any portion of God's inerrant letter to man.

The Difficulty of Unlearning What We Have Learned Incorrectly

As a kid, in my parents' back yard, I taught myself to shoot a basketball. Because I had no formal teacher, I practiced my shot based on what felt right and seemed reasonable, even logical. But these guidelines are insufficient if one's goal is to play with the best of the best. When I reached the professional level, I viewed my shot as normal until I observed how the greatest players in the world released a basketball. Then I knew that my shooting technique had to change or I would soon be out of a job. In the process, I discovered the difficulty of unlearning what I had learned incorrectly. This principle applies to all aspects of life, even to one's view of God and His Word.

If God is to change our improper thinking, patience and perseverance are required.   Therefore, are you willing to examine God's Word, study some highly debated subjects in context, based on all of the Scriptures rather than a select few,

I discovered the difficulty of unlearning what I had learned incorrectly.

and trust God to change your theology if what is discovered disproves something you previously believed? In other words, can we reason together, with God's truth as our standard, and trust Him to extract from our minds that which is theologically incorrect? This principle is exactly what the Lord had in mind while speaking through Isaiah:

"Come now, and let us reason together" (Isaiah 1:18)

People cannot reason together, by means of intelligent discussion, if absolutes are not permitted to affect their thought processes. Absolutes allow man to detect contradictions. In fact, absolutes reveal contradictions. Consequently, we will use the absolutes of God's Word to examine some of the more prevalent schools of thought of our day. If, of course, you do not view the Scriptures as containing valid instruction for proper living, we have no common ground on which to have a reasonable discussion. I understand this mindset better than you might imagine. I lived my first twenty-seven years perceiving God and His Word not only as

10

incapable of being understood, but also lacking the authority to properly direct one's life.

Two Well-Known Schools of Thought

Two well-known schools of thought, Calvinism and Arminianism, have greatly impacted how many believers, and even some unbelievers, define predestination, election, foreknowledge, etc. The scope of influence of these schools is vast, yet they many times use the same Scriptures to defend their diametrically opposed systems of thought. Both cannot be true when their teachings, based on the same Scriptures, are dissimilar. Is either correct? We will attempt to answer this question as we proceed.

A Third School of Thought

A third school of thought, postmodernism, also impacts the minds of many. Postmodernism, a secular mindset, rejects the existence of absolutes.

A Few Honest Questions

With the above in mind, please consider the following questions.

1. Who has your ear? Is it either Calvinism or Arminianism? If so, why do you deem that particular system of thought the bearer, possessor, and owner of the truth?

2. Is what you have learned from Calvinism or Arminianism (or both) based on absolutes, allowing the full counsel of God's Word (all of the verses instead of a select few) to eliminate any doctrine that is contradictory in nature?

3. Has our postmodern society convinced you that what you believe need not be void of contradiction? If so, you are presently at the mercy of a system, or teacher, instead of the truth of the Scriptures. This predicament must be remedied immediately if you desire to, first, properly view Who God is and, second, properly portray Him to others.

Detecting the Counterfeit

How individuals are trained to detect counterfeit dollar bills ties in well here. They are given the real thing, a real dollar bill, and instructed to look (gaze) at the bill until bills with even the slightest variance are recognizable at first sight.

This series is intended as an aid in detecting counterfeit interpretations of the Scriptures down to the slightest variance. If two of the major schools within Christendom, Calvinism and Arminianism, cannot agree doctrinally, many times using the same verses to attempt to prove their diametrically opposed positions, what are you going to believe? Do you just throw up your hands and conclude that God is such a mystery that He cannot be understood at all? Also, if you have decided to line up with one of these two schools, what, or who, convinced you to do so? In fact, what has caused you to believe anything that you believe regarding the Father and His selfless Son, Jesus Christ? If your answer is something other than God's Word, studied in context, and based on the full counsel (every word, phrase, verse, chapter, and book), you have answered incorrectly. The sad part is that so long as your answer is anything other than the contextual, full counsel view of God's Word, you will be at the mercy of every charismatic, energetic, and passionate teacher who crosses your path. Has the Spirit of God yet convinced you that passionate people are sometimes wrong? Passion is not the litmus test that confirms and legitimizes the truth! The apostle Paul confirmed this fact <u>before</u> his conversion by how zealously he persecuted Christians. The only legitimate litmus test is whether what is being stated or written is void of contradiction when placed beside the inerrant Word of God.

I can be wrong; you can be wrong; everyone can be wrong—besides the Godhead. Consequently, do not believe anything you hear (or read) in this study unless it is in agreement with every word, phrase, verse, chapter, and book included in the Scriptures. Should any portion of what is taught contradict the truth, disregard it. I suggest, however, that you read the entire study before drawing your final conclusions. What may seem contradictory initially might prove to be non contradictory in the end. If a portion of what is written becomes confusing, just continue reading. Future input will probably bring understanding

Repetition, Repetition, Repetition

I repeat myself quite often. In fact, repetition (stating the same principle in a variety of ways) is commonplace from beginning to end. I also use parenthetical expressions (some of which are lengthy) for the sake of clarification. Also, phrases such as, "repent and believe while depraved," and, "from eternity past by means of an eternal decree," are used so often that they will probably become burdensome. However, they are vital for clarity due to the theological shift occurring within

Christendom. Consequently, make sure to read all sentences in their entirety, even those which seem wordy, redundant, and prolonged.

Separating the Revealed from the Secret

Some people have questioned the need for further discussion regarding the topics addressed in this series because they are weary of the subject matter. Others are so confused that they think a solution to the "madness" is unachievable. As a result, a trend is developing that greatly concerns me, a trend that labels nagging inconsistencies as "secret things." Let me explain.

Moses recorded the following:

> *The secret things belong to the LORD our God, but the things revealed belong to us and to our sons forever....,* (Deuteronomy 29:29)

Two facts can be extracted from this verse:

1. God possesses *"secret things"* that belong to Him alone.

2. God has *"revealed"* certain things to man.

We must be careful, therefore, not to allow any of God's *"secret things"* to be classified as things that are *"revealed."* For instance, we can in no way presently comprehend the intricacies of how God spoke into existence the sun, moon, stars— in fact, any of creation. That knowledge belongs to Him alone, but I trust that He will share a portion of this secret once we see Him face to face. If not, He knows best. We will be perfectly satisfied with what we are privileged to understand, no matter how little or much.

We, at the same time, must guard against classifying *"the things"* that have been *"revealed"* as *"The secret things"* of God. We become lazy-minded when this mentality is allowed to rule, many times belittling those who seek answers to that which we have incorrectly categorized as impossible to grasp.

Incorrectly Classifying Contradiction as Mystery

We will discover that many people classify contradiction as "mystery" in an attempt to justify their system of thought. This practice is very unwise. Prudence, on the other hand, allows God's Word to eliminate all contradiction, leaving the truth, and nothing but the truth, in its wake.

First Button in the First Buttonhole

Allowing God's Word to expose all contradictions reminds me of an illustration that I once heard from a very humorous, but extremely wise man. He said that if the top button on a shirt is placed in an improper buttonhole, the man wearing the shirt will never resemble anything but a fool.

Taking the illustration a little further, suppose that a man had been taught that it was proper, and according to the blueprint of the designer, to place the first button in the second buttonhole of a button-down-shirt. His buttoning technique, obviously, would have been in contradiction to the designer's original blueprint. Suppose, however, that he instructed others to mimic his technique and to train additional individuals to do the same—the resulting numerical growth confirming, in their minds at least, that their teaching was correct. Together, they all had a great time, wondering why the majority could not agree with their methodology. They, obviously, overlooked one key matter. When the first button on a shirt is placed in the second buttonhole and all of the subsequent buttons are fastened one hole off, the bottom button has no available buttonhole but the first. Imagine a button-down-shirt wearer strolling around town with the bottom button of his shirt raised to meet the top buttonhole. He/she would be classified as foolish, silly, senseless, crazy, or maybe even insane. Contradiction, therefore, cannot be concealed when one's improper methodology is taken to the bottom button. In other words, because contradiction generated at the beginning grows exponentially until the end, the true litmus test of any system of thought is where it starts and finishes.

Allow God's Word to expose all contradictions.

Suppose that one day the designer of the button-down shirt happened by and, seeing the contradictory buttoning technique, began to describe the purpose of his "invention." He stated that not only was it designed to provide warmth and covering but comfort as well. He even presented his original blueprint and explained how and why the first button was to be placed in the first buttonhole, with each button following in proper sequence.

Suddenly, those who had buttoned their shirts incorrectly had a decision to make. They could either undo the first button that had been placed in the second buttonhole, place it in the first buttonhole, and admit their error, or continue to button their shirts as they were accustomed, first button in the second buttonhole. However, they could never teach anyone else, at least with a clear conscience (or without speaking or writing an overabundance of words in an attempt to justify their improper methodology), that the designer designed the shirt to be buttoned with the first button in the second buttonhole. Would they not have carried guilt as well for misrepresenting the innocent designer's intentions? After all, the designer ultimately gets the blame if a garment brings shame to its possessor.

The moral to the story is: When the first button is placed in an inappropriate buttonhole, many words are required to attempt to explain how the technique could be proper and according to design. Differences can be subtle, but extremely damaging to the designer's reputation. These subtle differences can also damage the reputation of those who choose to button incorrectly, especially when their methodology is placed beside the designer's original blueprint.

The Value of a Proper Starting Point

The previous illustration confirms that an improper start can yield an undesirable finish.   In the same vein, the movie, *National Treasure,* is a wonderful representation of a critical spiritual principle. The main character in the movie pursues a treasure more valuable than anything in the material realm. Yet, a problem exists. Because a number of skilled treasure hunters had sought the treasure to no avail, they concluded that it had ceased to exist (or never existed at all). Nevertheless, the hero of the movie possessed the courage to think outside the box. In doing so, he discovered that the Declaration of Independence had to be stolen from its well-guarded chamber in Washington, D.C. After all, a map revealing the location of the treasure was sketched on the back of the document. He also realized that a special pair of eyeglasses was required to view and interpret the map. These eyeglasses, hidden in a totally different location, were found only through following a series of complex and extremely vague clues.

As I watched the movie, I was intrigued by how much this treasure hunter had to know about history, and a wealth of other subjects, to follow the cryptic, difficult clues. He also had to lay down the contradictory ideology of his fraternity of treasure hunters (associates), for their pursuits had failed due to one common miscalculation: Each began his/her hunt from the wrong geographical location. In other words, they placed the first button in an improper buttonhole. They had done what felt right, and even seemed logically correct. However, their conclusions were in disagreement with the ultimate guideline—the map on the back of the Declaration of Independence.

*H*e had to lay down the contradictory ideology of his associates.

Once the hero of the movie had secured the Declaration of Independence and the special eyeglasses, another issue had to be addressed.   The glasses were equipped with an additional pair of lenses, and both pairs (one over the other) had to be engaged to properly interpret the map. Only with the assistance of these eyeglasses, both pairs of lenses in operation, could the treasure be found.

The object lesson is that a proper view of God's heart is the ultimate treasure. To find it requires a map viewed through a special pair of eyeglasses. The map is the Word of God. The eyeglasses are a principle coupled with a Person. The principle is the contextual view of the Scriptures (the first pair of lenses), and the Person is the Holy Spirit (the second pair of lenses). One will not work independently of the other, for the Holy Spirit will never lead anyone into a violation of the contextual view of the Scriptures. Neither will the contextual view of God's Word teach anything in disagreement with God's Spirit, for neither God nor anything related to Him is a contradiction.

As I think of the possibilities available through this series, I realize the risk involved in addressing this subject matter. I faced a similar situation while teaching the *Romans 1-8* study several years ago. God had revealed some truths from that portion of His Word that have revolutionized my life, so I taught them realizing that many persons in attendance might be in disagreement. Sure enough, some individuals strongly opposed the message, but the good news is that God has used those truths to bring about significant change in the lives of several of His saints. In fact, I doubt that this ministry would exist today had God not revealed that Paul's words of Romans 1-8 (which include the truth regarding the eradication of the old man and the awesomeness of the believer's identity) are much needed instruction if one is to place the first button in the first buttonhole of his/her theology. However, I will admit that it seemed, at times, as though we were as radical in our thinking as the man who chose to steal the Declaration of Independence.

My prayer is that my inabilities will not prevent you from hearing the message (note that I used the word "hearing" and not "believing"). As was stated earlier, you are not required to believe anything you are taught in this study. Nonetheless, please consider what is communicated, even if you should struggle with the content of the message. If, after taking what you have read through all the verses, chapters, and books in God's Word, you should find contradiction, I would welcome your input. I want to hear every argument against what I believe regarding any theological matter. Consequently, in preparing for this series, I have listened to more messages and read more materials from teachers who differ with me than from those who agree. The last thing I want to do is shelter what I believe from any opposing view. After all, if what I deem to be truth contains error (contradiction), it will do me harm so long as it goes undetected. It would be equivalent to placing the first button in an improper buttonhole, ultimately bringing shame to the Creator.

Subjects to be Addressed

The *God's Heart* series consists of four books. These four books are listed below:

1. *God's Heart as it Relates to Foreknowledge/Predestination*

2. *God's Heart as it Relates to Sovereignty/Free Will*

3. *God's Heart as it Relates to Depravity*

4. *God's Heart as it Relates to Election/Atonement/Grace/Perseverance*

This book, *God's Heart as it Relates to Foreknowledge/Predestination*, addresses several subjects but focuses primarily on foreknowledge and predestination. A portion of these subjects is addressed below along with some of the most common beliefs associated with each. Understand, therefore, that what is recorded here is not exhaustive as to what people believe regarding these topics.

Depravity

1.   Some people perceive the depraved (the spiritually unregenerated) as incapable of exercising personal repentance and faith. In fact, they believe that God must spiritually regenerate the depraved and give them the gifts of repentance and faith <u>before</u> they can repent, exercise faith, and be saved/justified. In this case, spiritual regeneration <u>precedes</u> repentance, faith, and salvation/justification.

2.   Others perceive the depraved as capable of exercising personal repentance and faith. In this case, repentance and faith <u>precede</u> spiritual regeneration (salvation/justification). Those who hold to this view normally perceive God as drawing the depraved to Himself in the midst of their depravity (John 6:44; 12:32; 16:8) without providing the decisive impulse that determines whether they will or will not repent and believe. Should the depraved choose to repent and believe, God's drawing assists them in their coming to Himself. However, the <u>decisive</u> impulse (choice) is left to the one desiring salvation (Acts 16:31, John 1:12, etc.)—not to God.

Which mindset is correct? We will allow the Scriptures to decide.

17

Sovereignty

1. Some people believe that God's sovereignty is compromised should man possess a free will—especially in the area of choosing where he will spend eternity. They believe that if man's choices could violate God's will, that man would be more sovereign than God.

2. Others believe that God's sovereignty makes room for man to possess a free will, even in the area of exercising personal repentance and faith while depraved.

Which system of thought is in agreement with all of the Scriptures, rather than a select few viewed from an improper context? We will pursue the answer with much diligence as this series unfolds.

Predestination

1. Some people perceive God as having looked into the future (by means of His eternal foreknowledge), and in response, elected to salvation (by means of an eternal decree) those who choose to repent and believe while depraved. This school normally teaches that the depraved, the spiritually unregenerated, possess a free will and can choose to repent and believe.

2. Others view God as having predestined the "elect" to salvation and the "non-elect" to damnation from eternity past by means of an eternal decree (with no dependence on His foreknowledge). They also perceive the depraved as incapable of exercising personal repentance and faith.

3. Other individuals perceive God as having predestined the "elect" to salvation (from eternity past, by means of an eternal decree—with no dependence on His foreknowledge), while having given the non-elect over to the consequence of their sin. They also perceive the depraved as incapable of exercising personal repentance and faith.

4. Another school of thought perceives God as having predestined the "elect" to salvation (from eternity past) by means of an eternal decree (with no dependence on His foreknowledge), yet giving mankind a free will to repent and believe while depraved.

5. Others perceive New Testament believers as predestined when they exercise personal repentance and faith while depraved and, through the avenue of the Holy Spirit (1Corinthians 12:13), are placed in Christ and made new (2Corinthians 5:17). These persons view God as predestining New Testament believers to blessings once they are in Christ, subsequent to their repenting and believing while depraved, rather than having predestined the "elect" to salvation from eternity past by means of an eternal decree.

Does Scripture agree with any of these views? We will find out shortly, so don't allow the number of options to dishearten you. Predestination is extremely simple when taken through the full counsel of God's Word.

Election

1. In some cases, election is perceived as God having elected certain individuals to salvation from eternity past by means of an eternal decree.

2. Other individuals perceive election as pointing to the special office or position that every New Testament believer receives through exercising personal repentance and faith while depraved and becoming a *"new creation"* in Christ (2Corinthians 5:17; 1Corinthians 12:13). Note: If the terms "office" or "position" confuse you, realize that they point to the special gifting that the New Testament believer receives in conjunction with being made new in Christ (1Peter 4:10). You will become very familiar with these terms as we proceed.

Which view, according to the Scriptures, is correct? We will diligently pursue the answer to this monumental question as this study progresses.

Note: The phrase, "New Testament believer," points to believers who live during the church age, an age which began in Acts 2 and will continue through the Rapture of the church.

The Believer's Chosenness

1. In some cases, the believer's chosenness is perceived as God having chosen certain individuals to salvation from eternity past by means of an eternal decree.

   2. Others perceive the believer's chosenness as pointing to the special office or position that every New Testament believer receives through exercising personal repentance and faith while depraved and becoming a *"new creation"* in Christ (2Corinthians 5:17; 1Corinthians 12:13).

Note that election and the believer's chosenness are one and the same. Thus, the words "elect" and "chosen" are synonymous, often being interchanged in the Scriptures. As a result, when we study election as an independent topic, we will also be addressing the New Testament believer's chosenness.

Foreknowledge

   1. Some individuals view foreknowledge, not as God foreknowing what will occur due to His omniscience, but rather as God foreordaining (or causing) everything that transpires. In other words, they perceive God as knowing future events only because He (according to their view) causes all events.

   2. Others perceive God as foreknowing (foreseeing) everything that occurs, before it occurs, because of His omniscience—not because He causes everything that transpires. In other words, they believe that God is <u>not</u> required to cause all things to know all things.

We will soon discover what the Scriptures teach regarding the subject.

The Hardening of Pharaoh's Heart

   1. Some students of the Scriptures perceive Pharaoh's heart as having been hardened by God to prevent him from obeying.

   2. Others view God as having hardened Pharaoh's heart through giving Pharaoh the courage and strength to carry out what Pharaoh had freely chosen.

We will soon discover what God's Word teaches concerning the matter and have much fun in the process.

Faith

1. One system of thought advocates that God spiritually regenerates the elect, void of a choice on their part, and then gives them the faith to believe and be saved. This system views the depraved as incapable of choosing to believe. In this arrangement spiritual regeneration precedes God's gift of faith, and is then followed by belief and salvation.

2. Others teach that the faith exercised by those seeking salvation does not find its origin in the Godhead, but is generated by the depraved prior to spiritual regeneration. This school of thought views spiritual regeneration as synonymous with salvation/justification. In this case, faith is exercised by the depraved with spiritual regeneration (God's gift of salvation) following.

What do the Scriptures teach regarding faith? We will allow them to speak for themselves as we proceed.

The Key

With such a variety of views from which to choose, the thought of placing the first button in an improper buttonhole warrants concern. After all, the views listed above vary because they each start with a different premise, idea, or presupposition. In other words, they have their first buttons in different buttonholes. For this reason, we will allow God's Word to determine which button is the first button, and in what buttonhole it belongs—especially as we study predestination, election, one's chosenness, foreknowledge, and other related topics.

We need access to the key—the starting point that unlocks the proper meaning of these terms. In other words, we need our own personal copy of the map located on the back of the Declaration of Independence along with the accompanying specialized eyeglasses.

The following subject matter will need to be read more than once (maybe several times) for proper understanding. Don't become discouraged, therefore, your first time through. Also note that the same truth is stated in a variety of ways. Repetition can be a valuable tool when properly implemented. Hopefully, it has been properly implemented in this application.

Our search will begin by determining what the Scriptures communicate regarding God's purposes, decrees, and works. These subjects, defined correctly, are vital because they reveal the proper definition of foreknowledge—the first button in the appropriate buttonhole.

We will start by confirming that God is *"eternal"*:

> *"The eternal God is a dwelling place, And underneath are the*
> *everlasting arms; And He drove out the enemy from before you,*
> *And said, 'Destroy!'* (Deuteronomy 33:27)

> *For a child will be born to us, a son will be given to us; And the*
> *government will rest on His shoulders; And His name will be*
> *called Wonderful Counselor, Mighty God, Eternal Father, Prince*
> *of Peace.* (Isaiah 9:6)

> *but now is manifested, and by the Scriptures of the prophets,*
> *according to the commandment of the eternal God, has been made*
> *known to all the nations, leading to obedience of faith;* (Romans
> 16:26)

> *Now to the King eternal, immortal, invisible, the only God, be*
> *honor and glory forever and ever. Amen.* (1Timothy 1:17)

> *how much more will the blood of Christ, who through the eternal*
> *Spirit offered Himself without blemish to God, cleanse your*
> *conscience from dead works to serve the living God?* (Hebrews
> 9:14)

Based on Acts 15:18, God has always (eternally) known His *"works."*

> *Known unto God are all his works from the beginning of the world* (Acts
> 15:18 KJV).

> *Known to God from eternity are all His works* (Acts 15:18 NKJV).

God's *"works"* are the natural byproduct of His purposes. If no purpose exists, no work can occur. Because God's purposes are *"eternal"* (Ephesians 3:11; 2Timothy 1:9), He has always known them; they have always existed within His heart:

> *This was in accordance with the eternal purpose which He carried*
> *out in Christ Jesus our Lord,* (Ephesians 3:11 NASB)

> *who has saved us, and called us with a holy calling, not according*
> *to our works, but according to His own purpose and grace which*

> *was granted us in Christ Jesus from all eternity,* (2 Timothy 1:9
> NASB)

Scripture confirms, therefore, that an eternally known work requires an eternally known *"purpose."* Because the same Greek word used for *"eternal"* in Ephesians 3:11 is used to describe the eternal King of the universe in 1Timothy 1:17, we can know that God's purposes are eternal as well.

> *Now unto the King eternal, immortal, invisible, the only wise God,*
> *be honour and glory for ever and ever. Amen.* (1Timothy 1:17
> KJV)

This truth explains Paul's use of the words, *"eternal purpose,"* in Ephesians 3:11. According to Job 22:28 and Daniel 11:36b, the function of a *"decree"* is to establish the certainty of the fulfillment of God's purpose:

> *"You will also decree a thing, and it will be established for*
> *you;...*(Job 22:28 NASB)

> *"Then the king will do as he pleases, and he will exalt and magnify*
> *himself above every god, and will speak monstrous things against*
> *the God of gods; and he will prosper until the indignation is*
> *finished, for that which is decreed will be done.* (Daniel 11:36
> NASB)

Undoubtedly, if no *"decree"* exists, no purpose can be fulfilled, and no work can follow.

God's purposes are *"eternal"* (Ephesians 3:11; 2Timothy 1:9) because they have always existed within His heart. In addition, His decrees, which guarantee the certainty of the fulfillment of His purposes, are also *"eternal,"* as confirmed by Jeremiah 5:22:

> *'Do you not fear Me?' declares the LORD.' Do you not tremble in*
> *My presence? For I have placed the sand as a boundary for the*
> *sea, An eternal decree, so it cannot cross over it. Though the*
> *waves toss, yet they cannot prevail; Though they roar, yet they*
> *cannot cross over it.* (Jeremiah 5:22 NASB)

Isaiah 63:16 verifies the eternalness of God's decrees mentioned in Jeremiah :22, for God's *"name"* (Isaiah 63:16), which is eternal, has existed *"from everlasting"*—*"from everlasting"* (Isaiah 63:16) and *"eternal"* (Jeremiah 5:22) being from the same Hebrew word:

...thou, O LORD, art our father, our redeemer; thy name is from everlasting. (Isaiah 63:16 KJV)

The same Hebrew word is rendered *"Eternal"* in Genesis 21:33 (AMP) as well:

Abraham planted a tamarisk tree in Beersheba and called there on the name of the Lord, the <u>Eternal</u> God. (Genesis 21:33 Amplified Bible)

Certainly, God is *"Eternal,"* with no beginning or end.

Conclusion: God's eternal decrees, which make certain the fulfillment of His eternal purposes, bring to fruition His eternally known works. Obviously, if God's decrees are eternal, they have always existed. Because foreknowledge means "to know beforehand," God can't foreknow an eternal decree due to its eternalness. In other words, God can't foreknow what has no beginning. Thus, God has never said, "I knew before I decreed this decree that I would decree it," because His decrees have always existed within His heart. Dave Hunt agrees:

> There is no point in saying that God foreknew His eternal decrees—nor could He. Since <u>His decrees have always been</u>, and thus were never future to Him, there is no way in which He could know what they would be before they were decreed. (*What Love Is This?* p. 283)[1]

Hunt quotes John Wesley, confirming that Wesley perceived God's decrees as eternal:

> God decrees, <u>from everlasting to everlasting</u>, that all who believe in the Son of his love, shall be conformed to his image.... (*What Love Is This?* p. 287)[2]

Even John Calvin spoke of the eternal nature of God's decrees:

> By predestination we mean the <u>eternal decree of God,</u> by which he determined with himself whatever he wished to happen with regard to every man. (*Institutes*: Book 3; Chapter 21; Section 5)[3]

> We say, then, that Scripture clearly proves this much, that God by <u>his eternal and immutable counsel</u> determined once for all those whom it was his pleasure one day to admit to salvation, and those

whom, on the other hand, it was his pleasure to doom to destruction. (*Institutes*: Book 3; Chapter 21; Section 7)[4]

This input ("key") should greatly affect our perception of foreknowledge. Considering that a proper view of foreknowledge is the first button in the first (and proper) buttonhole, the following should encourage anyone desiring to base his/her theology on all the Scriptures rather than a select few.

Foreknowledge: A Major Player

Foreknow is from the Greek word *pro-ginosko*—*pro* meaning "previous" and *ginosko* meaning "knowledge." Consequently, foreknow means "to know beforehand in the sense of foreseeing." Warning: Understanding this section (**Foreknowledge: A Major Player**) is absolutely essential, but a few readings may be necessary to fully comprehend its content.

Scripture confirms that God's decrees are eternal, as was verified earlier. Because God's decrees are eternal, and have never been future to Him, He couldn't have foreknown them. Why? Even God can't foreknow what has no beginning. Eternity past would need a starting point should God's foreknowledge have preceded any of His eternal decrees. (Refer to Diagram 2, "Why God's Foreknowledge Cannot Precede His Eternal Decrees," located in the Reference Section.)

Had God's foreknowledge ever preceded eternity past, eternity would have ceased to be eternity. Why? By definition, eternity has no beginning or end. In other words, if eternity had a starting point, it could no longer be called eternity and God, Whom the Scriptures portray as eternal, would be non-existent.

Due to the impossibility of God foreknowing His decrees because of their eternalness, for Him to have predestined or elected individuals to salvation by means of an eternal decree is nonsensical. The following paragraph explains why this is the case, so be sure to comprehend its content before continuing.

Both the predestination (Romans 8:29 NASB) and election (1 Peter 1:1-2 KJV) of the New Testament believer are <u>according to</u> foreknowledge, not foreknowledge according to predestination and election. This means that foreknowledge must precede the predestination and election of a New Testament believer. As a result, predestination and election can never be the reason for His foreknowledge. He <u>never</u> foreknows, in other words, because He has predestined or elected.

Conclusion: Foreknowledge means "to know beforehand in the sense of foreseeing." God has never foreknown that a person would accept Christ due to having predetermined, from eternity past (by means of an eternal decree), his or her destiny. And, in cases where foreknowledge cannot apply, the predestination and

25

election of a believer cannot transpire. After all, foreknowledge must precede the New Testament believer's predestination and election according to passages such as Romans 8:29 (NASB) and 1Peter 1:1-2 (KJV)—a fact substantiated even more so later in this *God's Heart* series.

What, then, is predestination and election? When do they occur? The Scriptural answer to these questions will be obtained when predestination and election are studied independently. The journey will be challenging but amazingly fruitful.

The "Key" Refutes Calvinism and Arminianism

Utilizing our "key," addressed earlier, let's collect ourselves for a moment and reflect on what we have discovered. We have proven that the predestination and election of New Testament believers cannot occur in situations where God's foreknowledge cannot apply, because the predestination and election of church saints are according to (they follow, in other words) His foreknowledge.

> *For whom He foreknew, He also predestined to become conformed*
> *to the image of His Son, that He might be the first-born among*
> *many brethren;* (Romans 8:29)
>
> *Elect according to the foreknowledge of God the Father,....* (1Peter
> 1:2 KJV)

These verses confirm that believers could not have been predestined or elected to salvation by means of an eternal decree due to the simple fact that God's decrees have always existed. Consequently, such a scenario would leave no room for God's foreknowledge to precede the New Testament believer's predestination and election. Predestination and election, therefore, cannot point to God selecting, or decreeing, certain individuals to salvation by means of an eternal decree—refuting all forms of Calvinism and Arminianism.

Further Contradiction within Calvinism and Arminianism

Calvinism and Arminianism view God's eternal decrees as sequential, one following the other (note Diagram 12 in the Reference Section). However, for an eternal decree to follow an eternal decree would mean that the one following would have a beginning—a total impossibility. This subject is discussed in great depth in *God's Heart as it Relates to Depravity*, the third book of this four-book series.

The Futility of Redefining Terms

We have confirmed that some systems of thought attempt to prove from the Scriptures that believers have been elected and predestined to salvation (from eternity past) by means of God's eternal decrees. They do so by taking the liberty to redefine foreknowledge and foreknow as foreordination and foreordain, or predestination and predestine. Their goal is to make foreknowledge equivalent to foreordination or predestination, but Romans 8:29 clearly makes a distinction, proving them to be different (*"for whom He foreknew, He also predestined..."*— Romans 8:29). This rearrangement of the meaning of foreknowledge to be equivalent to foreordination or predestination not only defies common sense, but also totally violates the rules of proper Biblical interpretation.

We cannot change the meaning of terms in an attempt to validate an unscriptural experience or system of thought. In fact, we should never allow our experience or system of thought to dictate what we accept or reject regarding God's Word. Rather, we should always allow God's Word to dictate what we accept or reject regarding an experience or system of thought. Scripture is never to be at the mercy of a particular way of thinking, but all ways of thinking are to be at the mercy of the Scriptures. Thus, we cannot allow anyone or anything to compel us to change the definition, or meaning, of any term addressed in God's holy Word.

We cannot change the meaning of terms in an attempt to validate a contradictory system of thought.

Consider the following illustration as an example of the chaos that can follow random definition and word replacements.

A Sure Way to Degrade an Honorable Reputation

(The information contained in the first two paragraphs of this section can be found online while searching for "invention of basketball." The illustration which follows pretends that phones were in existence when the game of basketball was invented in 1891.)

James Naismith, a PE teacher at the University of Massachusetts, invented basketball in 1891 with two peach baskets, attached to a 10-foot-high railing, and a soccer ball, inside a YMCA in Massachusetts. He formulated the first rules in 1892. Initially, players dribbled a <u>soccer</u> ball up and down a court of varying dimensions. Points were earned by shooting the ball into a peach basket. Iron hoops and a hammock-style basket were introduced in 1893. Open-ended nets were invented ten years later, finally eliminating the need to remove the ball from the basket each time a goal was scored. <u>Soccer</u> balls were used for some time before official basketballs came on the scene. U.S. patent #1,718,305 was granted on June 25, 1929 for the basketball now used in the game.

"Football" is the name given to a number of team sports, all of which involve, to varying degrees, kicking a <u>ball</u> with the foot in an attempt to score a <u>goal</u>. The most popular of these sports (internationally) is "associational <u>football</u>," more commonly known as "<u>football</u>" or "<u>soccer</u>."

What if, back in 1891, when the game of basketball was being played with a <u>soccer</u> ball, a man in the United States, named Michael, who was absolutely fascinated with this new game, phoned a friend named Ian, in Europe, and described it to him to the best of his abilities? He had little time to talk, so the conversation was intense and very much to the point. He described a participant dribbling a soccer ball and shooting it at a goal.

His friend in Europe, due to having never seen a basketball game, could only interpret Michael's words through the grid of his own personal experiences—which caused him to miss the word "dribbling" altogether. In fact, he assumed that his friend in America had described the game of football (football being a synonym for soccer in Europe). Ian was delighted that Michael could be so excited about his European game, the game of soccer, or football. Yet, Ian viewed Michael as somewhat confused after Michael called soccer, "basketball." Ian incorrectly assumed, therefore, that all his friend needed was to replace the word "basketball" with the word "soccer" (or "football") and went on his merry way.

One day, another man in America, named Larry, who had never heard of the game of basketball or the American game called football, was given an official football for his birthday. He appreciated the gift but spent much time trying to decide how a sport could be played with such a strange object. After all, it was oval shaped, much like an egg. If you tried to roll it, it responded strangely. If you attempted to bounce it off the floor or wall, it was a frightening experience indeed. No telling which direction the ball would carom!

Shortly afterwards, Larry received a call from the European gentleman (Ian) who was, of course, eaten up with soccer—loved soccer, "ate soccer and slept soccer"— the sport which he called "football." The American, Larry, told him about the football he had received and asked if Ian knew with what game it might be associated. Due to the busyness of his day, Ian began to quickly describe the game of soccer (football in Europe). He began telling Larry that the ball was made to be kicked into a net at the end of a grassy field. He also, in passing, told him about his friend, Michael, who had, by Ian's estimation, called the game of football "basketball." After making this statement, Ian exited the conversation, leaving Larry with just enough information to be totally ill-informed.

Soon afterwards, Larry overheard some men talking about a game they called basketball—a first for him. Larry, remembering the conversation with Ian from

Europe and Ian's statements regarding Michael's "error," calling "football" (in Ian's estimation) by the improper name, "basketball," assumed the men were misguided as well.

Larry was preoccupied with the events of his day, but the men made a statement that could not be disregarded. It seemed strange to Larry, but he heard them say that someone was "dribbling" a basketball. After all, the men, in Larry's mind at least, were mistaken about the name of the game. In his estimation they had incorrectly called the game "football," "basketball," for clearly they had also stated that a ball had been shot at a goal.

Suddenly, our story becomes extremely interesting. What if Larry, in the midst of his lack of knowledge of the game of basketball, decided to make it his mission in life to convince every American that the game (basketball) should be renamed "football"? If he did so, however, he would be required to replace the word "ball" with "football" in every instance in Naismith's original rulebook. He would also have to describe how a football could be dribbled. Imagine the degree of difficulty involved in such an undertaking! The books would be limitless in number because his argument would be based on a contradiction—his redefining the name of the game. Because context is everything, words defined out of context reap horrible results.

How could the word "football," should it replace the word "ball," fit into the original intent of the inventor of the game of basketball? Let's take a moment to ponder that thought by looking at just the first four rules recorded in James Naismith's original <u>basketball</u> rulebook, replacing "ball" with "football":

1. The <u>ball</u> [football] may be thrown in any direction with one or both hands.
2. The <u>ball</u> [football] may be batted in any direction with one or both hands, but never with the fist.
3. A player cannot run with the <u>ball</u> [football]. The player must throw it [the football] from the spot on which he catches it, allowance to be made for a man running at good speed.
4. The <u>ball</u> [football] must be held by the hands. The arms or body must not be used for holding it [the football].

These four rules could somewhat apply to football, but not totally. However, the fifth rule blows Larry's theory through the roof:

5. No shouldering, holding, pushing, striking or tripping in any way of an opponent. The first infringement of this rule by any person shall count as a foul; the second shall disqualify him until the next goal is made or, if there was evident intent to injure the person, for the whole of the game. No substitution shall be allowed.

The bottom button of Larry's argument reveals the magnitude of his error. Consequently, the only way Larry could convince anyone that his rulebook was legitimate would be to classify its multitude of contradictions as "mystery," trusting that his ideology would never be challenged. This practice sounds like something that could survive only within the confines of a postmodern society—a society that welcomes contradictions at the expense of absolutes.

If someone desired to destroy the game of basketball, the solution would be simple. Convince enough people that a basketball should be replaced with a football on the streets of Chicago, New York, Los Angeles, and the dirt courts of rural America, and basketball would be exterminated in a heartbeat. The degree of difficulty would be so great that no one would desire to participate. The saddest part, should Larry's error be accepted as truth, is that James Naismith would be perceived as a man who had lost his way. However, remove the contradictions from Larry's new rulebook by reassigning the proper ball to Naismith's original intent, and the inventor of "basketball" is totally vindicated.

Basketball was designed to be a very simple game. A ball, in the shape of a sphere, was to be dribbled by a participant until an opening was found—from which the ball was shot into a circular basket. Minimal brainpower is required to understand the concept of the game. (Maybe that is why it so grabbed me as a kid.) In fact, some of the greatest basketball players in America are not presently playing in the National Basketball Association (NBA). They are still "doing their thing" in the streets due to allowing their passion for the game to supersede their passion for the classroom. Yet, all that would be required to reduce this heightened craving would be to redefine some key terms associated with the game. I guarantee you that if the word "football" should be allowed to replace the word "ball" in the inventor's original rulebook, the game would become extinct. Players contemplating participating would never give it a second thought.

The bottom line of this illustration is that redefining the terms within any rulebook severely damages that to which the rulebook applies, grossly misrepresenting, in the process, the original intent of its author—thus diminishing his reputation in the end. James Naismith would have been grossly misguided and rightly accused had he selected an oval football as the ball of choice for the game he so wonderfully designed. One could only imagine the number of contradictions involved had someone desired to change the word "ball" (basketball) to "basket weaving."

The proper definition of foreknowledge is as vital to understanding predestination, election, and the believer's chosenness as the proper ball is to the game of basketball—even more so, in fact. In addition, a healthy view of foreknowledge helps one properly

A healthy view of foreknowledge helps define other vital theological matters.

define a host of other vital theological matters. Consequently, we must never accept the idea that foreknowledge can be redefined, as some theologians have incorrectly assumed, for the purpose of perpetuating a contradictory presupposition.

Holding the Teacher Accountable

God's Word has withstood the scrutiny of man since its inception. If man, with unwavering passion, has held God accountable for what He has recorded, man should be held accountable for what he teaches or writes regarding God's Word. I should be held accountable, and you should be held accountable. In fact, everyone should be held accountable for what he/she communicates concerning "the truth." As we discuss the topics addressed during our time together, the different schools of thought will be held accountable for what they espouse. The question we must ask ourselves is: Are we willing to accept what agrees with Scripture and reject what does not? If we are unwilling to discard that which contradicts God's Word, no basis exists from which we can *"reason together"* (Isaiah 1:18) in our pursuit of the truth.

We have confirmed the impossibility of God's foreknowledge preceding any of His eternal decrees because it would mean that eternity has a beginning, thus eliminating eternity altogether (refer to Diagram 2, "Why God's Foreknowledge Cannot Precede His Eternal Decrees" included in the Reference Section). Thus, God could <u>not</u> have predestined, elected, or chosen anyone to salvation by means of an eternal decree because God's foreknowledge could not have preceded God's actions in such an arrangement.

We will discover how uncomplicated and downright simple predestination, election, and the believer's chosenness are when properly linked to God's foreknowledge. These topics will then be studied independently and in great depth. In the process we will observe the futility of redefining foreknowledge as foreordination or predestination.

God's Omniscience

The Scriptures have much to say regarding Who God is. He, from His elevated position above the earth (Isaiah 40:22), can view all events from eternity past through eternity future throughout His eternal existence. This ability confirms that He is not controlled by time (2Peter 3:8). Time was created for man—not God Who transcends time. No wonder God stated to Moses, *"I AM WHO I AM"* (Exodus 3:14), and Jesus avowed, *"before Abraham was born, I Am"* (John 8:58). God is the eternal present tense. He sees all things at once, making Him the Omniscient One, the all-knowing One, described so vividly in the Scriptures.

Observe Diagram 3, "God, The Eternal I AM," included in the Reference Section. Note that God sits above the earth, viewing all events that transpire throughout His eternal existence. Consequently, what occurred two thousand years ago, along with what will transpire during the future Millennial reign of Christ, is constantly before Him. He sees all future events, therefore, as though they have already occurred. How can this be? Because He transcends time, there is no past or future to Him. In fact, everything is present tense to the Godhead. This is why Jesus could say, *"before Abraham was born, I Am"* (John 8:58). The Second Person of the Trinity, being God (Hebrews 1:8), is the eternal present tense—not "I was" or "I will be," but the eternal *"I am."* Of course, all three Persons of the Trinity are God: God the Father, God the Son, and God the Holy Spirit.

On page 286 of his work, *What Love Is This?*, Dave Hunt quotes John Wesley as follows:

> When we speak of God's foreknowledge we...speak...after the manner of men. For...there is no such thing as either foreknowledge or after knowledge in God. All...being present to him at once, he does not know one thing before another, or one thing after another; but sees all...from everlasting to everlasting. As all time, with everything that exists therein, is present with him at once, so he sees at once, whatever was, is or will be to the end of time. But observe; we must not think they are, because he knows them. No; he knows them because they are.[5]

God truly is amazing, seeing all things at once from eternity past through eternity future throughout His eternal existence. As a result, He is the present tense *"I Am"* (Exodus 3:14; John 8:58). Thus, in relation to future events, as man perceives them, God's knowledge of all things is viewed as His foreknowledge. This truth ties in well with the following input.

On page 183 of *What Love Is This?*, Dave Hunt also quotes Michael J. Kane from *Christianity Today.* As we continue, note that wording is sometimes inserted between brackets [ ] for clarification. Underlines are also used for emphasis:

> The actual existence of past, present, and future is required by Einstein's theory of relativity. All space and time form a four-dimensional continuum that simply exists; the theory does not permit time to be treated as a dimension in which the future is open or incomplete.
>
> From a Christian point of view, it is reasonable to conclude that the temporal and the spatial extent of our universe were created together, and thus the entire four-dimensional structure resides

before [in view of] its Creator in an eternal present. Thus our modern scientific understanding of the nature of time fits quite well with the Christian tradition that <u>God has knowledge of all time, past, present, and future</u>: "Before Abraham was, I am."[6]

Einstein's Dilemma

Hugh Ross, on pages 73-74 of his work, *The Creator and the Cosmos*, writes the following regarding Einstein as he (Einstein) was confronted with the fact that his theory of relativity had proven that the universe had a "Beginner":

Einstein's "superior reasoning power," however, was not the God of the Bible. Though he confessed to the rabbis and priests who came to congratulate him on his discovery of God that he was convinced God brought the universe into existence and was intelligent and creative, he denied that God was personal.

Of course, those clergy had a stock response to Einstein's denial: How can a Being who is intelligent and creative not also be personal? Einstein brushed past their objection, a valid one, by raising the paradox of God's omnipotence [His unlimited power] and man's responsibility for his choices: If this Being is omnipotent, then every occurrence, including every human action, every human thought, and every human feeling and aspiration is also His work; how is it possible to think of holding men responsible for their deeds and thoughts before such an almighty Being? In giving out punishment and rewards He would to a certain extent be passing judgment on Himself. How can this be combined with the goodness and righteousness ascribed to Him?

None of the clergy Einstein encountered ever gave him a satisfactory answer to his objection. Typically, they responded by saying that God has not yet revealed the answer. They encouraged him to endure patiently and blindly trust the All-Knowing One.

Regrettably, Einstein lacked the perseverance to pursue an answer further. He took for granted the biblical knowledge of those religious professionals and assumed that the Bible failed to adequately address the crucially important issue. Of what value, then, could such a "revelation" be?

> Lacking a solution to the paradox of God's predestination and human beings' free choice, Einstein, like many other powerful intellects through the centuries, ruled out the existence of a personal God. Nevertheless, and to his credit, Einstein held unswervingly, against enormous peer pressure, to belief in a Creator.
>
> I am grieved that no one ever offered Einstein the clear, biblical resolution to the paradox he posed. I am also sad that Einstein did not live long enough to see the accumulation of scientific evidence for a personal, caring Creator. These might have sparked in him a willingness to reconsider his conclusions.[7]

The solution to Einstein's dilemma lies in a proper view of foreknowledge, predestination, election, and the believer's chosenness. This *God's Heart* series is committed to making these extremely profound subjects amazingly simple. We hope you are blessed by its content!

The Simplicity of Predestination

New Testament believers are predestined to receive a glorified body once they are placed in Christ after repenting and believing while depraved. (Note that words and phrases are sometimes underlined for emphasis in certain verses throughout the remainder of this study.)

Explanation:

God's foreknowledge must precede the predestination of a New Testament believer:

> *For whom He foreknew, He also predestined to become conformed to the image of His Son, that He might be the first-born among many brethren;* (Romans 8:29)

Predestination, therefore, as it relates to church saints, must point to something other than God predetermining man's destiny from eternity past. (Note Diagrams 2, 7 and 8 in the Reference Section.) In fact, in Ephesians 1:5 we find that New Testament believers are *"predestined...to adoption as sons"*:

> *He predestined us to adoption as sons through Jesus Christ to Himself, according to the kind intention of His will,* (Ephesians 1:5)

The phrase, *"adoption as sons,"* points to that time when church saints will receive their glorified bodies, verified by Paul in the book of Romans:

> *And not only this, but also we ourselves, having the first fruits of the Spirit, even we ourselves groan within ourselves, waiting eagerly for* <u>*our adoption as sons, the redemption of our body.*</u> (Romans 8:23)

We can conclude, therefore, that New Testament believers are predestined, not to salvation from eternity past, but to blessings at the time they are born anew after repenting and believing while depraved. Church saints, in conjunction with being placed in Christ and receiving eternal life (subsequent to exercising personal repentance and faith while depraved), are predestined to be the beneficiaries of great blessings. This interpretation allows God's foreknowledge to precede that time when a New Testament believer receives his/her glorious future destiny in conjunction with being placed in Christ and made new. (Reference Diagrams 2, 7, and 8 if necessary.) Consequently, being predestined prior to new birth is impossible, new birth occurring once we are placed in Christ (2Corinthians 5:17) after repenting and believing while depraved. When we study predestination in greater depth, we will dissect every verse where *"predestined"* is used to make certain that our conclusions are based on the full counsel of God's Word.

The Simplicity of Election

New Testament believers are elected/chosen once they are placed in Christ, placed in God's elected/chosen Son (Luke 9:35; Isaiah 42:1), after repenting and believing while depraved.

Explanation:

Like predestination, election is easily understood. The words "elect" and "chosen" are synonymous, as is evidenced by the fact that 1Peter 1:1-2 in the NASB states *"chosen"* while the KJV uses *"Elect"*:

> *Peter, an apostle of Jesus Christ, to the strangers scattered throughout Pontus, Galatia, Cappadocia, Asia, and Bithynia, <u>Elect</u> according to the <u>foreknowledge</u> of God the Father, through sanctification of the Spirit, unto obedience and sprinkling of the blood of Jesus Christ: Grace unto you, and peace, be multiplied.* (1Peter 1:1-2 KJV)

> *Peter, an apostle of Jesus Christ, to those who reside as aliens, scattered throughout Pontus, Galatia, Cappadocia, Asia, and Bithynia, who are <u>chosen</u> according to the <u>foreknowledge</u> of God the Father, by the sanctifying work of the Spirit, that you may obey Jesus Christ and be sprinkled with His blood: May grace and peace be yours in fullest measure.* (1Peter 1:1-2 NASB)

The following reveals that a New Testament believer is chosen/elected when he/she is placed in Christ through the power of the Holy Spirit after repenting and believing while depraved. This fact will be confirmed to a greater degree when we address the contextual view of passages such as Ephesians 1:4.

From 1Peter 1:1-2, we discover that New Testament believers, church saints, are *"chosen* [elected] *according to the foreknowledge of God."* Since the Scriptures require God's *"foreknowledge"* to precede that time when a New Testament believer is *"chosen"* (elected), church saints could not have been *"chosen"* (elected) to salvation from eternity past by means of an eternal decree. (If this statement is somewhat confusing, a quick glance at Diagrams 1, 2, 3, 7 and 8 in the Reference Section should bring clarification). Just as it is with predestination, the New Testament believer's chosenness (election) must be preceded by God's foreknowledge of man's thoughts, decisions, actions, and works (1Peter 1:1-2). Consequently, church saints are chosen/elected once they are placed in Christ through God's Spirit (1Corinthians 12:13) after repenting and believing while depraved (leaving ample room for God's foreknowledge to precede such an arrangement)—Christ being the Father's *"chosen one"* (Luke 9:35; Isaiah 42:1):

> *"This is My Son, <u>My Chosen One</u>; listen to Him!"* (Luke 9:35)

> *"Behold, My Servant, whom I uphold; My <u>chosen one</u> in whom My soul delights. I have put My Spirit upon Him; He will bring forth justice to the nations.* (Isaiah 42:1)

Jesus was chosen by the Father, but not to salvation. He was chosen to office, the office of Messiah. Thus, when we were placed in Christ subsequent to repenting and believing while depraved, we were placed in the *"chosen one"* of

Luke 9:35 and Isaiah 42:1, Jesus Himself. To what were we chosen once we were placed in Him? We were chosen to office, for all New Testament believers receive a special gift (office) in conjunction with being placed in the Father's *"chosen one"*:

> *As each one has received a special gift, employ it in serving one another, as good stewards of the manifold grace of God.* (1Peter 4:10)

This special gift is similar to the disciples' chosenness. The disciples were <u>not</u> chosen to salvation, but rather to apostleship (John 6:70)—an office that could be accepted or rejected, as verified by Judas' betrayal (John 6:70).

No doubt, foreknowledge, predestination, and election (the believer's chosenness) can be relatively easy to comprehend. Later, when we study these topics independently and in much greater depth, we will realize how complicated they become when certain schools of thought redefine "foreknowledge" as "foreordination" or "predestination."

The Big Question: Must God Cause all Things to Know all Things?

God is never caught off guard, meaning that He is never required to make a hurried decision to remedy an unforeseen state of affairs. With this in mind, we must answer a very important question. Must God cause all things to know all things? If we answer correctly, we are well on our way to properly understanding not only God's foreknowledge, but what the Scriptures teach regarding predestination, election, the believer's chosenness, God's sovereignty, and a host of other highly debated theological issues. Because we will study these topics over an extended period of time, you will have ample opportunity for the subject matter to take root and bear fruit. Each topic will be examined from a Scriptural basis as well as from the vantage point of the differing views within Christendom. You will note that the views from the different schools of thought, and not the Scriptures themselves, have brought confusion to so many within Christ's body. The profound should become extremely simple as we pursue answers to some of the most debated topics of our day.

PART THREE ❧ CHAPTER THREE

FOREKNOWLEDGE

NOW, WE EMBARK on our in-depth study of foreknowledge, which will add great depth and flavor to the introduction. An accurate perception of foreknowledge is mandatory for viewing predestination, election, the believer's chosenness, and a host of other highly debated topics, from a proper frame of reference. Foreknowledge, defined according to the full counsel of God's Word, is the first button in the first, or proper, buttonhole. In other words, if foreknowledge is defined incorrectly, the Creator's reputation suffers much harm. Yes, it is that important!

The Greek word *proginosko*, from which we get terms such as *"foreknew"* and *"foreknow,"* simply means "To know beforehand in the sense of foreseeing." An important usage of this word in New Testament Scripture relates to God's ability to foreknow the thoughts, decisions, actions, and works of man.

Diagram 3, "God, The Eternal I Am," located in the Reference Section, illustrates that God sees all things from eternity past through eternity future throughout His eternal existence. He is totally omniscient, knowing all things before they occur. From this truth the question arises: Must God cause all things to know all things? This question, along with several others, will be answered as we seek to properly define this most critical term.

Diagrams 1, 2, and 3, located in the Reference Section, present in graphic form what the Scriptures teach regarding foreknowledge. These diagrams will be used extensively as we examine every New Testament usage of the Greek *prognosis*, from which we get the English "foreknowledge."

Some systems of thought view foreknowledge as equivalent to foreordination or predestination by supposing that God predetermines man's destiny before man is born (we will observe the flaw in this mindset shortly). But, what did the early church fathers believe regarding the subject? After all, they, desiring to perpetuate the teachings the apostles received from Christ, proclaimed the gospel soon after the apostles' death.

The Early Church Fathers' View of Foreknowledge

I recently heard two men discussing foreknowledge on a local radio program. They confidently stated that to reject their view would be equivalent to rejecting what the apostles and early church fathers believed regarding the subject. They then began mocking anyone who refuses to perceive foreknowledge as a synonym for foreordination or predestination. In other words, they wrongly assumed that foreknowledge could be redefined as foreordination or predestination. As I listened, I wondered what percentage of their audience could detect the error in their message. It reminded me of Paul's words to Timothy regarding false teachers in 1Timothy 1:6-7. Their *"confident assertions"* could not have been more misguided, for they grossly contradicted the words of the early church fathers from 100 AD to approximately 250 AD. Note the following, with words underlined for emphasis:

Clement of Rome—Died traditionally 99 or 101 AD.

> 2 Clement 9:9 "For he foreknoweth all things, and knoweth the things that are in our hearts." (Forster and Marston, *God's Strategy in Human History*, page 191)[8]

Clement, obviously, did not say that God foreordained all things.

Justin Martyr—Converted to Christianity about A.D. 130, taught and defended the faith in Asia Minor and Rome, where he suffered martyrdom about the year 165 AD.

> "For He foreknows that some are to be saved by repentance, some even that are perhaps not yet born. In the beginning He made the human race with the power of thought and of choosing the truth and doing right, so that all men are without excuse before God; for they have been born rational and contemplative." (*First Apology*; Chapter 28)[9]

> "So that what we say about future events being foretold, we do not say it as if they came about by a fatal necessity; but God foreknowing all that shall be done by all men...." (*First Apology*; Chapter 44)[10]

> "And that God the Father of all would bring Christ to heaven after He had raised Him from the dead, and would keep Him there until He has subdued His enemies the devils, and until the number of those who are _foreknown_ by Him as good and virtuous is complete, on whose account He has still delayed the consummation..." (*First Apology*; Chapter 45)[11]

> "...that God, wishing men and angels to follow His will, resolved to create them free to do righteousness; possessing reason, that they may know by whom they are created...,But if the word of God foretells that some angels and men shall be certainly punished, it did so because it foreknew that they would be unchangeably [wicked], but not because God had created them so." (*Dialogue*; Chapter 141)[12]

Origen—185-254 A.D.

> "I shall take from the Scriptures the predictions regarding Judas, or the foreknowledge of our Savior regarding him as the traitor...Celsus [a pagan philosopher who wrote between the years 175 and 180 AD] imagines that an event, predicted through foreknowledge, comes to pass because it was predicted; but we do not grant this, maintaining that he who foretold it was not the cause of its happening, because he foretold it would happen;" (*Argument Celsus*; Book II; Chapter 20)[13]

These early church fathers viewed God as possessing foreknowledge, which they defined as "God's ability to know beforehand." They also rejected the idea that God must cause all things to know all things. Because they learned about foreknowledge from the writings of the apostles, they had no need to redefine foreknowledge as foreordination or predestination. The erroneous doctrine that portrays God as having predetermined the believer's destiny by means of an eternal decree was not present in their time. An open and honest examination of church history reveals no other conclusion.

Roger T. Forster and V. Paul Marston, on page 192 of *God's Strategy in Human History*, state:

> We can find no hint in any of the early church writings that "foreknow" was ever interpreted in the sense of the theologians whose views are cited in note 2.[14]

("Note 2" cites theologians who lived <u>after</u> the departure of the <u>early</u> church fathers and viewed foreknowledge as equivalent to foreordination or predestination.)

These examples refute the false teaching that the early church fathers viewed foreknowledge as a synonym for foreordination or predestination. In fact, redefining the term did not gain popularity until later.

Calvinism's Struggle with Foreknowledge

Foreknow always means "to know beforehand in the sense of foreseeing." The fact that foreknowledge must precede election and predestination has presented an array of problems for individuals who suppose that God has chosen/elected and predestined to salvation, by means of an eternal decree, those who will be saved. In actuality, foreknowledge, when allowed to retain its proper meaning, totally refutes such thinking. In an attempt to remove this impasse, some theologians go so far as to redefine foreknowledge as foreordination or predestination. However, many individuals within this group portray God as not only having predetermined man's destiny <u>from eternity past</u>, but also the cause of all things. After all, if man were incapable of choosing his own destiny, as many Calvinists (and all Reformed theologians) believe, God would be required to make the choice for him (study Diagrams 10 and 11 in the Reference Section to understand how the terms "Calvinism" and "Reformed Theology" relate).   They then take this false presupposition and expand it, concluding that God is the cause of everything that transpires.

John Calvin (1509-1564 AD) believed that God could only foreknow what He caused. In other words, he viewed God as having to cause all things to know all things. Note the following quote from Calvin's *Institutes*:

> If God merely foresaw human events, and did not also arrange and dispose of them at his pleasure, there might be room for agitating the question, how far his foreknowledge amounts to necessity; but since he foresees the things which are to happen, simply because he has decreed that they are so to happen, it is vain to debate about prescience, while it is clear that all events take place by his sovereign appointment. (*Institutes*: Book 3; Chapter 23; Section 6)[15]

R.C. Sproul (a Reformed theologian), in *Almighty Over All,* (pp. 52-54) writes:

> God wills all things which come to pass...; God...desired that man
> would fall into sin...; God...created sin.[16]

If God willed all things, then God could be blamed for everything—every sin, sickness, disaster, tragedy, misfortune, failure, heartache, and anything else man could imagine. How, then, could He judge those whom He caused to sin? In doing so He would be totally unjust and, therefore, anything but the righteous, just, and loving God portrayed so vividly in the Scriptures.

If God willed all things, He could also be viewed as having elected the elect to salvation from eternity past, by means of an eternal decree, with man having no choice in the matter. No Scriptural proof exists for this idea. Even so, John MacArthur (a Reformed theologian) writes the following in *The Love of God*, page 17:

> God's love for the elect is an infinite, eternal, saving love. We
> know from Scripture that this great love was the very cause of our
> election (Eph. 2:4). Such love clearly is not directed toward all of
> mankind indiscriminately, but is bestowed uniquely and
> individually on those whom God chose in eternity past.[17]

MacArthur references Ephesians 2:4 in an attempt to prove that God's love is the cause of the believer's election to salvation "in eternity past" (rather than election to office in conjunction with being saved—what I deem to be the proper view). Ephesians 2:4, when studied in context with its surrounding verses, does not teach MacArthur's view. In fact, Scriptural proof does not exist for God's election of any believer to salvation "in eternity past." MacArthur's unhealthy evaluation of sovereignty, that God must be the cause of all things, brings him to this erroneous conclusion.

Calvinism's Limited Omniscience

Omniscience points to God's ability to know all things. However, if God must cause all things to know all things, as many Calvinists believe, He is less omniscient than the Scriptures indicate. For instance, Jesus cited fulfilled prophecies from the Old Testament to validate His Messiahship to the two men traveling to Emmaus:

> *And beginning with Moses and with all the prophets, He explained
> to them the things concerning Himself in all the Scriptures.* (Luke
> 24:27)

Jesus' respect for the Old Testament prophets is demonstrated in this passage. He had fulfilled (through yielding to the Father) a wealth of prophecies during His First Coming and freely expressed this truth to His two companions. But, would the two men have been less impressed with the Father's accomplishments through the Son had they viewed God as the cause of all things, leaving man void of a will to choose as he pleased? They would have, and the following illustration confirms why.

Free Will and God's Omniscience

Suppose that on a beautiful spring day two men who claimed to be God approached a college student on his way to class. One man was a skilled surgeon with an ability to implant computer chips into animals for the purpose of programming their behavior. The other man claimed to know in advance the behavior of every animal on the earth. The college student desired to embarrass the two men in the midst of their folly, so he concocted a test. He gave each man 100 dogs from a local animal shelter, a shelter that had cared for the animals remarkably well. The surgeon received 100 brown dogs with numbered collars, while the other gentleman received 100 black dogs with numbered collars. Both men were asked to predict the exact time that each dog, once released, would find his or her way back to the comfortable shelter. The surgeon took his 100 dogs and implanted a computer chip in each. The other man did nothing but turn his dogs loose, freeing them to choose as they pleased. The following day all 200 dogs arrived at the animal shelter at the exact times specified by the two men. If the student were foolish enough to believe that man could be God, which man would he pick? It wouldn't be the surgeon!

Think about it. God's omniscience would be diminished should He cause all things.

Foreknowledge and Calvin's View of Predestination

As a result of redefining foreknowledge as foreordination or predestination, and avoiding the fact that foreknowledge must precede the predestination of a New Testament believer, Calvin, in addition to teaching that God is the cause of all things, also taught that God predestined the elect to salvation, from eternity past, by means of an eternal decree (underline for emphasis in the following quotes):

> By predestination we mean the <u>eternal decree of God</u>, by which he determined with himself whatever he wished to happen with regard to every man. All are not created on equal terms, but some are preordained to eternal life, others to eternal damnation; and,

43

accordingly, as each has been created for one or other of these ends, we say that he has been predestinated to life or to death. (*Institutes*: Book 3; Chapter 21; Section 5)[18]

We say, then, that Scripture clearly proves this much, that God by his eternal and immutable counsel determined once for all those whom it was his pleasure one day to admit to salvation, and those whom, on the other hand, it was his pleasure to doom to destruction. We maintain that this counsel, as regards the elect, is founded on his free mercy, without any respect to human worth, while those whom he dooms to destruction are excluded from access to life by a just and blameless, but at the same time incomprehensible judgment. In regard to the elect, we regard calling as the evidence of election, and justification as another symbol of its manifestation, until it is fully accomplished by the attainment of glory. But as the Lord seals his elect by calling and justification, so by excluding the reprobate either from the knowledge of his name or the sanctification of his Spirit, he by these marks in a manner discloses the judgment which awaits them. (*Institutes*: Book 3; Chapter 21; Section 7)[19]

...that God, by an eternal decree, fixed the number of those whom he is pleased to embrace in love, and on whom he is pleased to display his wrath, and that he offers salvation indiscriminately to all. I hold that they are perfectly consistent, for all that is meant by the promise is, just that his mercy is offered to all who desire and implore it, and this none do, save those whom he has enlightened. Moreover, he enlightens those whom he has predestinated to salvation. Thus the truth of the promises remains firm and unshaken, so that it cannot be said there is any disagreement between the eternal election of God and the testimony of his grace which he offers to believers. (*Institutes*: Book 3; Chapter 24; Section 17)[20]

Scripture verifies that foreknowledge must precede the predestination (Romans 8:29) and election (1Peter 1:1-2) of New Testament believers (note Diagram 2 in the Reference Section). But, if church saints were predestined and elected to salvation by means of an eternal decree, as Calvinism supposes, God's foreknowledge could precede neither. Consequently, Calvinism's elect could not have been predestined and elected to salvation by means of an eternal decree as Calvin suggested.

The Simplicity of Predestination and **The Simplicity of Election**, located in the **Introduction**, explain how New Testament believers are predestined and elected to blessings in conjunction with God making them new rather than predestined and elected to salvation from eternity past, by means of an eternal decree, as Calvinists, Reformed theologians, and Arminians incorrectly assume.

Arminius' Struggle with Calvin's Extremes

James Arminius (1560-1609 AD), who at one time followed the teachings of Calvin, observed the contradictions in Calvin's theology relating to depravity and the free will of man. Calvin held the view that man is so depraved that he cannot choose to repent and believe. According to Calvin, God predetermined, by means of an eternal decree, the destiny of all men and women (refer to Diagram 6 in the Reference Section). Calvin also portrayed God as the cause and author of evil. Arminius, who viewed unregenerate man as depraved but possessing the ability to choose to repent and believe, set out to refute Calvin's teachings. Thus, Arminius, differing with Calvin, believed that the depraved are free to choose Christ.

Arminius' Beliefs

Arminius disagreed with Calvin in other areas as well. As was discussed earlier, Calvin's view of foreknowledge incorporated the idea that God had to cause all things to know all things. Arminius' view of foreknowledge allowed God to foreknow the future without causing it.

Like Calvin, Arminius believed that "the elect" were elected and predestined to salvation from eternity past, by means of an eternal decree. But unlike Calvin, he viewed this election and predestination as contingent upon God's eternal foreknowledge (refer to Diagrams 4 and 5 in the Reference Section). In *The Works of James Arminius*, Arminius states:

> To these succeeds the fourth decree, by which God decreed to save
> and damn certain particular persons. This decree has its foundation
> in the <u>foreknowledge</u> of God, by which he knew <u>from all eternity</u>
> those individuals who would, through his preventing grace,
> believe, and, through his subsequent grace would persevere,
> according to the before described administration of those means
> which are suitable and proper for conversion and faith; and, by
> which <u>foreknowledge</u>, he likewise knew those who would not
> believe and persevere. *(The Works of James Arminius;* Volume 1;

> Translated from the Latin by James Nichols; *On Predestination;*
> *My Own Sentiments on Predestination)*[21]

Arminius believed that God looked into the future and, by means of His eternal foreknowledge, saw who would choose to repent and believe while depraved. God then, based on Arminius' theology, chose (elected) and predestined them to salvation from eternity past by means of an eternal decree (reference Diagram 4, "Arminius' Beliefs"). This train of thought, on the surface at least, seems to make election and predestination dependent on His foreknowledge—as required by Scripture. However, the full counsel of God's Word reveals that Arminius' theology contradicts Scripture.

Foreknow means "to know beforehand in the sense of foreseeing." According to Romans 8:29 and 1Peter 1:1-2, foreknowledge must precede the New Testament believer's predestination and election. Arminius stated in the previous quote that God's decree "has its foundation in the foreknowledge of God." He also stated that God's foreknowledge is eternal, yet believed that God elected and predestined the elect to salvation from eternity past by means of an eternal decree. However, if all of God's decrees (Jeremiah 5:22) are eternal, how could God's foreknowledge precede His decrees? It could not! (For more input, reference Diagram 5.) Consequently, Arminianism and Calvinism are both in error by concluding that believers were elected and predestined to salvation by means of an eternal decree. If believers were elected and predestined to salvation by means of an eternal decree, room would not exist for God's foreknowledge to precede election or predestination, as is required by passages such as Romans 8:29 and 1Peter 1:1-2. (Note Diagram 2 in the Reference Section titled, "Why God's Foreknowledge Cannot Precede His Eternal Decrees.")

Arminius committed the same critical error as Calvin. He confused the blessings associated with salvation with salvation itself. New Testament believers were not predestined and elected/chosen to salvation from eternity past, by means of an eternal decree. They are predestined and elected/chosen to blessings in conjunction with being made new in Christ—after repenting and believing while depraved. These blessings will be studied in depth as we progress.

Conclusions to be Drawn from Arminius' Beliefs

Arminius, although once a follower of Calvin, eventually rejected Calvinism due to its extremes. Arminius' major problem with the excesses of Calvinism centered on its fallacious assumption that unregenerate man is so depraved that he is incapable of repenting and believing (a view presently espoused by extreme and hyper Calvinism, or Reformed Theology), which eliminates free will altogether—especially in relation to the depraved choosing Christ. It, in turn, makes God the

46

cause of all things, even evil. Arminius could not accept this skewed view of Jehovah.

Neither could Arminius accept that Calvinism's predestination and election were not dependent on God's foreknowledge. Arminius believed that God's foreknowledge is "from all eternity." Thus, he viewed it as an eternal foreknowledge that need not be redefined as foreordination or predestination—a redefinition consistently implemented by extreme and hyper-Calvinists (Reformed theologians).

Arminius' view of foreknowledge affected his view of salvation. He believed that God looked into the future and, by means of His eternal foreknowledge, saw who would repent and believe while depraved. God then, based on his (Arminius') ideology, elected (chose) and predestined these future believers to salvation from eternity past by means of an eternal decree (read Arminius' earlier quote; also reference Diagram 4 in the Reference Section, "Arminius' Beliefs"). But, election and predestination do not pertain to salvation/justification, as was verified earlier in our study. Election and predestination pertain to the blessings associated with the salvation we received once we were placed in Christ—after we chose to repent and believe while depraved. In other words, we were not predestined and elected until we were made new in Christ (note Diagram 8 in the Reference Section).

*W*e were not predestined and elected until we were made new in Christ.

We observed earlier that predestination (Romans 8:29) and election (1Peter 1:1-2) must be preceded by God's foreknowledge. We observed as well that all of God's purposes (Ephesians 3:11; 2Timothy 1:9) and decrees (Jeremiah 5:22) are eternal (review **The Key** in the **Introduction**). If every decree of God is eternal, and God's foreknowledge is eternal, Arminius' view of the believer's election and predestination to salvation by means of an eternal decree must be incorrect because it leaves no room for God's foreknowledge to precede such an arrangement (reference Diagram 5). Verses such as Romans 8:29 and 1Peter 1:1-2 require that God's foreknowledge <u>precede</u> the predestination and election of all church saints. Arminius' error was failing to realize that predestination and election cannot point to God having selected certain persons to salvation from eternity past by means of an eternal decree—which, ironically, was also Calvin's Achilles heel.

47

The Remedy to Calvin and Arminius' Error

The remedy to Calvin and Arminius' error is realizing that God's foreknowledge (as it relates to passages such as Romans 8:29 and 1Peter 1:1-2) points to His foreknowledge of the thoughts, actions, decisions, and works of those who, during the church age, choose, while depraved, to repent and believe. (This, by no stretch of the imagination, means that God does not foreknow the thoughts, actions, decisions, and works of those who choose not to believe.) Once the depraved exercise repentance and faith and become, through God's power and grace, new creations in Christ (2Corinthians 5:17), He not only predestines them (grants them a glorious future destiny), but elects them to office as well (reference Diagram 8, "Scriptural Election/Chosenness and Predestination").

We must never confuse the blessings associated with salvation with salvation itself—a warning that both Calvin and Arminius failed to heed.

C H A P T E R   F O U R

REFORMED THEOLOGY'S UNWISE ATTEMPT TO REDEFINE FOREKNOWLEDGE

WE HAVE LEARNED that people who view God as having predetermined man's destiny before man is born, by means of an eternal decree (with the depraved incapable of repenting and exercising faith), must then view foreknowledge as equal to foreordination and predestination. This erroneous modification is an attempt to change the proper meaning of foreknowledge. After all, so long as "foreknowledge" means "foreknowledge" (to know beforehand in the sense of foreseeing), man must be capable of repenting and believing while depraved. No wonder John Piper, a Calvinist (Reformed theologian), wrote the following:

> God does not foreknow the free decisions of people to believe in
> him because there aren't any such free decisions to know. (*Piper
> and Staff "Tulip,"* 22).[22]

Piper and other followers of Reformed Theology (extreme and hyper-Calvinism) foster these beliefs when Scripture makes a clear distinction between foreknow, "to know beforehand in the sense of foreseeing," and foreordination and predestination. How they draw their conclusions is alarming and can be extremely confusing. Thus, if the following becomes unclear, don't be overly concerned. I repeat: <u>If the following becomes unclear, don't be overly concerned.</u> Understanding will come later. Glean what you can and move on.

The subject matter covered over the next few pages is in my opinion the most difficult of the entire *God's Heart* series. You should comprehend the usefulness of this input later in our study. However, if you become overwhelmed, just skip it and pick up with Chapter Five, titled **FOREKNOWLEDGE IN THE NEW TESTAMENT**. Let's begin.

Those who err, by equating foreknowledge with foreordination or predestination, and thus redefining the term, think along the following extremely contradictory lines:

1. They begin by incorrectly assuming that the Hebrew word *yada*, which is interpreted "know" in the Old Testament, can mean "choose." Verses such as Amos 3:2-3, Hosea 13:5, Genesis 18:17-19, and Jeremiah 1:5 are cited while attempting to validate their conclusions—all of which we will study shortly.

2. The Hebrew word *yada* ("know") is interpreted the majority of the time as *ginosko* in the LXX (the Septuagint—a Greek translation of the Hebrew Old Testament Scriptures). Those individuals who desire for foreknowledge to mean foreordination or predestination take this fact and incorrectly assume that if the Old Testament word *yada* ("know") can somehow mean "choice" (which it cannot), then the New Testament word *ginosko*, which is interpreted as "know," can mean "choice" as well.

3. The Greek word *proginosko*, from which we get the English word "foreknow," is made up of two parts. The first part is *pro*, meaning "previous," while the second is *ginosko*, meaning "knowledge." Those individuals who equate foreknowledge with foreordination and predestination take this fact and draw a final, yet improper conclusion: They incorrectly assume that if *ginosko*, meaning "knowledge," can mean "choice" (which it cannot), then *proginosko*, from which we get foreknow, can mean foreordination or predestination.

Pause for a moment to catch your breath. Remember that you were warned of the confusing nature of Reformed Theology's (extreme and hyper-Calvinism's) argument regarding its redefinition of foreknowledge as foreordination or predestination.

Reformed Theology's Argument Regarding *Yada* in Amos 3:2-3

We will examine this argument by first observing Amos 3:2-3, verses used by Reformed Theology (extreme and hyper-Calvinism) to draw the previous conclusions. I have underlined "*known*" and "*chosen*" in the following Scriptural references for emphasis:

> *You only have I <u>known</u> of all the families of the earth: therefore I will punish you for all your iniquities. Can two walk together, except they be agreed?* (Amos 3:2-3 KJV)

> *"You only have I <u>known</u> of all the families of the earth; Therefore I will punish you for all your iniquities." Can two walk together, unless they are agreed?* (Amos 3:2-3 NKJV)

> *You only have I <u>known</u> of all the families of the earth: therefore I will visit upon you all your iniquities. Shall two walk together, except they have agreed?* (Amos 3:2-3 ASV)

> *"You only have I <u>known</u> of all the families of the earth; therefore I will punish you for all your iniquities. "Do two walk together, unless they have made an appointment?* (Amos 3:2-3 RSV)

Note that the KJV, NKJV, ASV, and RSV all use the word *"known"* to describe God's relationship with the Hebrew people. Yet, the NASB uses *"chosen"*:

> *"You only have I <u>chosen</u> among all the families of the earth; Therefore, I will punish you for all your iniquities." Do two men walk together unless they have made an appointment?* (Amos 3:2-3 NASB)

The word *"known"* (KJV, NKJV, ASV, RSV), the correct rendering, is from the Hebrew word *yada*. The NASB, however, inserts *"chosen."* Yet, the word *"chosen"* is referenced as *"known"* in the margin of my NASB. Why? As we learned earlier, the Hebrew word *yada* is normally translated in the LXX (the Septuagint—a Greek translation of the Old Testament Hebrew Scriptures) as *ginosko*, meaning *"know."* It does not mean "choose." I trust, therefore, that all who read the NASB possess the wisdom to reference the margins!

The nation of Israel was, and is, God's *"chosen...people"* (Deuteronomy 7:6; 14:2). This fact cannot be denied. Yet, when Amos 3:2-3 is studied in context, one finds that the word *"known"* actually points to God's special relationship with the nation, <u>not</u> to the fact that Israel was chosen. Amos 2:10-13 confirms this point:

> *10 "And it was I who brought you up from the land of Egypt, And I led you in the wilderness forty years That you might take possession of the land of the Amorite. 11 "Then I raised up some of your sons to be prophets And some of your young men to be Nazirites. Is this not so, O sons of Israel?" declares the LORD. 12 "But you made the Nazirites drink wine, And you commanded the prophets saying, 'You shall not prophesy!' 13 "Behold, I am weighted down beneath you As a wagon is weighted down when filled with sheaves.* (Amos 2:10-13 NASB)

Yes, God's special relationship with Israel includes a choice. However, His relationship with the nation is much deeper than a choice, just as a marriage consists of more than a choice. In fact, the choice of a spouse is no guarantee that a special relationship will result, as proven by the present divorce rate. God's relationship with Israel has been special indeed. Even in the midst of her disobedience, she was granted the privilege of receiving God's glory, a privilege granted to no other nation (Exodus 24:17; Romans 9:3-4). Consequently, the phrase, *"You only have I known of all the families of the earth"* (Amos 3:2 KJV), emphasizes God's knowledge of Israel as a result of His special relationship with her—not His choice of her.

The phrase, *"Can two walk together, except they be agreed?"* (Amos 3:3), also validates that relationship, not choice, is the emphasis. Because a special relationship is much greater than a choice, the two cannot be equated. Consequently, any attempt to use Amos 3:2-3 to prove that the New Testament Greek word *ginosko* ("know") is equivalent to election or choice is unacceptable. Thus, *"known"* (Amos 3:2) points to God's special relationship with Israel. It does not mean election or choice.

Just continue to persevere. Things will become less complex shortly. Is it not amazing how Calvinism's improper presuppositions complicate the gospel? Yet, Paul viewed the gospel as quite simple:

> But I am afraid, lest as the serpent deceived Eve by his craftiness, your minds should be led astray from the simplicity and purity of devotion to Christ. (2Corinthians 11:3)

Reformed Theology's Argument Regarding *Yada* in Hosea 13:5

Hosea 13:5 is another Old Testament passage used by those who attempt to make the Hebrew *yada* (*"know"*) equivalent to election or choice. If *yada* is incorrectly translated as election or choice, then the Greek word *ginosko,* meaning "know," can be incorrectly equated with election or choice. Then *proginosko,* instead of meaning foreknow, can incorrectly be defined as foreordination or predestination. These translational leaps are unworkable, as the following examination of Hosea 13:5 demonstrates.

> I did know thee in the wilderness, in the land of great drought. (Hosea 13:5 KJV)

The overall emphasis of the book of Hosea is Israel's broken relationship with God, not His choice of her. It first addresses Israel's harlotry, then describes that glorious day when the nation will be reunited with her husband, Jehovah. God did choose Israel, but His choice of the nation is not the issue in the book of Hosea. After all, God's choice of Israel (the nation) occurred before her days *"in the"* particular *"wilderness"* addressed in Hosea 13:5. It also occurred before Israel spent time *"in the land of great drought,"* mentioned in Hosea 13:5 as well. The *"wilderness"* addressed in Hosea 13:5, the wilderness where she wandered for forty years, is where Israel lacked water for a season (Numbers 20:1-2) due to *"drought"* conditions.

> *1 Then the sons of Israel, the whole congregation, came to the* <u>wilderness of Zin</u> *in the first month; and the people stayed at Kadesh. Now Miriam died there and was buried there. 2 And there was* <u>no water</u> *for the congregation; and they assembled themselves against Moses and Aaron.* (Numbers 20:1-2)

The Scriptures confirm that God chose Israel at an earlier date and in a different wilderness, *"the wilderness of Sinai"* (Exodus 19:2), when He married the nation at the base of Mount Sinai (Horeb) in Exodus 24:1-8.

> *When they set out from Rephidim, they came to the* <u>wilderness of Sinai</u>*, and camped in the wilderness; and there Israel camped in front of the mountain.* (Exodus 19:2)

> *1 Then He said to Moses, "Come up to the LORD, you and Aaron, Nadab and Abihu and seventy of the elders of Israel, and you shall worship at a distance. 2 Moses alone, however, shall come near to the LORD, but they shall not come near, nor shall the people come up with him." 3 Then Moses came and recounted to the people all the words of the LORD and all the ordinances; and all the people answered with one voice, and said, "All the words which the LORD has spoken we will do!" 4 And Moses wrote down all the words of the LORD. Then he arose early in the morning, and built an altar at the foot of the mountain with twelve pillars for the twelve tribes of Israel. 5 And he sent young men of the sons of Israel, and they offered burnt offerings and sacrificed young bulls as peace offerings to the LORD. 6 And Moses took half of the blood and put it in basins, and the other half of the blood he sprinkled on the altar. 7 Then he took the book of the covenant and read it in the hearing of the people; and they said, "All that the LORD has spoken we will do, and we will be obedient!" 8 So Moses took the blood and sprinkled it on the people, and said, "Behold the blood of the covenant, which the LORD has made with you in accordance with all these words."* (Exodus 24:1-8)

This marriage (which took place in Exodus 24:1-8) occurred <u>before</u> she entered the forty years of wanderings in the *"wilderness, in the land of great drought"* addressed in Hosea 13:5. The fact that the Scriptures make a distinction between *"the wilderness of Sinai"* and *"the wilderness"* of the *"forty years"* of wanderings is confirmed by Numbers 10:12, Deuteronomy 2:7, and Numbers 20:1-2:

> *and the sons of Israel set out on their journeys from the <u>wilderness</u> <u>of Sinai</u>. Then the cloud settled down in the <u>wilderness of Paran</u>.* (Numbers 10:12)

> *For the LORD your God has blessed you in all that you have done; He has known your wanderings through this <u>great wilderness</u>. These <u>forty years</u> the LORD your God has been with you; you have not lacked a thing."'* (Deuteronomy 2:7)

> *1 Then the sons of Israel, the whole congregation, came to the <u>wilderness of Zin</u> in the first month; and the people stayed at Kadesh. Now Miriam died there and was buried there. 2 And there was <u>no water</u> for the congregation; and they assembled themselves against Moses and Aaron.* (Numbers 20:1-2)

The Hebrew people became a people through Abraham, Isaac, and Jacob; they became a nation at the base of Mount Sinai when God <u>chose</u> them as His wife and in turn, to serve as *"a kingdom of priests"* (Exodus 19:6; 24:1-8). This choice happened <u>before</u> their forty years of wilderness wanderings *"in the land of great drought"* (Hosea 13:5).

Note: God did <u>not</u> choose the Jews for salvation. God saves Jews <u>after</u> they exercise repentance and faith while depraved, just as He saves the Gentile (Romans 2:17-3:8). This subject is addressed in much detail later in this series.

What, therefore, can be concluded regarding the word *"know"* in Hosea 13:5? Follow closely.

The term *"know"* in Hosea 13:5 cannot be equated with choice because we have proven that God's special relationship with the nation, not His choice of the nation, is the emphasis in the book of Hosea. Consequently, *yada*, which in Hebrew means "know," cannot be equated with choice by throwing Hosea 13:5 into the mix. Neither can it point to election. Therefore, this verse does <u>not</u> support the idea that the New Testament *ginosko*, meaning "know," can mean the same as election or choice. Neither can it be used to prove that *proginosko*, meaning "foreknow," can be equated with foreordination or predestination.

Is your head above water, or are you drowning? Keep in mind that things will get easier as we progress. This input is necessary if our goal is a proper view of

God's heart coupled with an understanding of the incorrectness of the opposing schools of thought.

Reformed Theology's Argument Regarding *Yada* in Genesis 18:17-19

Reformed theologians also use Genesis 18:17-19 in their attempt to equate the Hebrew *yada*, "*know*," with choice.

> *17 And the LORD said, Shall I hide from Abraham that thing which I do; 18 Seeing that Abraham shall surely become a great and mighty nation, and all the nations of the earth shall be blessed in him? 19 For I <u>know</u> him, that he will command his children and his household after him, and they shall keep the way of the LORD, to do justice and judgment; that the LORD may bring upon Abraham that which he hath spoken of him. (Genesis 18:17-19— KJV)*

> *17 And the LORD said, "Shall I hide from Abraham what I am about to do, 18 since Abraham will surely become a great and mighty nation, and in him all the nations of the earth will be blessed? 19 "For I have <u>chosen</u> him, in order that he may command his children and his household after him to keep the way of the LORD by doing righteousness and justice; in order that the LORD may bring upon Abraham what He has spoken about him."* (Genesis 18:17-19 NASB)

Note that the KJV uses *"know"* (v.19), while the NASB inserts *"chosen."* Interestingly, *"chosen"* is referenced as *"known"* in the margin of my NASB. Even the RSV inserts *"chosen,"* while the ASV employs *"known."* Thus, verse 19 has suffered greatly at the hands of the translators. So, which is correct? Context is key, which will be examined at this time.

An in-depth study of Genesis 18:17-19 reveals that *"know"* (v.19 KJV) is the proper rendering rather than *"chosen"* (NASB). After all, the Lord's words of Genesis 18:17-19 were stated after He had promised Abraham and Sarah a son (vv.1-16), but previous to His visit to Sodom (read vv.20-33)—a visit that resulted in the destruction of the city (Genesis 19:1-29). The depth of friendship motivated the Lord to reveal His plans to Abraham, not the fact that Abraham was chosen as the father of the Jewish nation. Abraham was God's *"friend"* (Isaiah 41:8; James 2:23), and friends confide in one other (John 15:15). Thus the phrase, *"For I know him"* (Genesis 18:19 KJV), is the proper rendering rather than, *"For I have chosen him"* (NASB).

Reformed Theology's Argument Regarding *Yada* in Jeremiah 1:5

Jeremiah 1:5 is another verse cited by those who attempt to interpret the Hebrew *yada*, *"knew"* in this case, as choice.

> *"Before I formed you in the womb I <u>knew</u> you, And before you were born I consecrated you; I have appointed you a prophet to the nations."* (Jeremiah 1:5 NASB)

The fact that *"knew"* cannot mean choice in this context is demonstrated in Jeremiah 12:3:

> *But Thou <u>knowest</u> me, O LORD; Thou seest me; And Thou dost examine my heart's attitude toward Thee. Drag them off like sheep for the slaughter And set them apart for a day of carnage!* (Jeremiah 12:3 NASB)

The word *"knowest"* points to God's knowledge of Jeremiah's heart, meaning that God knew everything about him. Consequently, the Hebrew word *yada* (*"knew"*) in Jeremiah 1:5 also means a thorough knowledge of Jeremiah's inward being. Even the LXX (the Septuagint) translates *yada* (*"knew"*) in Jeremiah 1:5 by the Greek word *epistamai* which means "to understand," not the Greek word *ginosko*. Why would Jeremiah need to comprehend that God understood everything about him? Jeremiah questioned his calling in Jeremiah 1:6:

> *Then I said, "Alas, Lord GOD! Behold, I do not know how to speak, Because I am a youth."* (Jeremiah 1:6 NASB)

Jeremiah viewed himself as a poor communicator due to his youthfulness. But, God thoroughly understood Jeremiah's shortcomings when He called him, a fact that would encourage Jeremiah throughout his days of ministry.

We have confirmed that the word *"knew"* (Jeremiah 1:5) points to God's infinite knowledge of Jeremiah as a person. When did Jeremiah become a person? It occurred at conception in his mother's womb, *"Before"* he was *"formed...in the womb"* (Jeremiah 1:5)—a person is conceived before he/she is formed. Of course, God, in His infinite foreknowledge, had known from eternity past that Jeremiah would be born and serve as a prophet. However, God did not know Jeremiah as a person until he was conceived in his mother's womb. After all, for God to have a relationship with an idea is impossible. Thus, *"knew"* (Jeremiah 1:5) points to God's infinite knowledge of Jeremiah's person, not to his chosenness as a prophet—although he most definitely was chosen to be a prophet (*"I have appointed you a prophet to the nation"*—Jeremiah 1:5), an office he could have rejected had he desired. Consequently, this verse cannot be used in an attempt to equate know with choice.

The previous Scriptures are the primary Old Testament verses referenced by those who <u>attempt</u> to equate *yada* ("know") with choice. We have verified that *yada* ("know") can be translated as choice only if the verses are interpreted out of context, thus violating the laws of proper Biblical analysis.

Reformed Theology's View of *"Known"* in 1Corinthians 8:1-3

Individuals who desire to connect the Greek word *ginosko* ("*know*") with choice or election normally use two New Testament references as their main argument—1Corinthians 8:1-3 and Galatians 4:8-9. An examination of these verses, in context, will determine if they have a valid case. We will begin with 1Corinthians 8:1-3.

> *1 Now concerning things sacrificed to idols, we know that we all have knowledge. Knowledge makes arrogant, but love edifies. 2 If anyone supposes that he knows anything, he has not yet known as he ought to know; 3 but if anyone loves God, he is <u>known</u> by Him.* (1Corinthians 8:1-3 NASB)

Paul is saying that *"knowledge"* relating to *"things sacrificed to idols"* (v.1) need not make a person *"arrogant."* In fact, Paul teaches that pride in such matters proves that his/her *"knowledge"* is lacking. Loving God, which results in obedience and humility, is what matters. Those who love God are obviously believers and, therefore, *"known by Him"* (v.3) in a way that is not experienced by those who reject Christ. After all, the New Testament believer is placed into Jesus <u>after</u> he/she, while depraved, repents of sin and accepts Christ through faith (2Corinthians 5:17). Since Jesus is in the Father (John 14:11), and New Testament believers are in Jesus (Ephesians 2:6), then the Father must know the church saint intimately (as a child of the Kingdom)—unlike the unredeemed (who are alienated from God so long as they refuse to repent and believe while depraved).

K nown means known. It does not mean chosen or elected.

Consequently, instead of *"known"* (1Corinthians 8:3) meaning chosen or elected, it means *"known,"* as confirmed by the context.

Some systems of thought, obviously, view the believer as having been chosen or elected to <u>salvation</u> from eternity past by means of an eternal decree. But, as has already been confirmed, and will be confirmed to even a greater degree as we continue, the New Testament believer is chosen or elected to a special <u>office</u> (position) in conjunction with being placed in Christ subsequent to repenting and believing while depraved. This office is not insignificant, but one of great blessing. Thus, church saints are not chosen or elected until the Holy Spirit places them in Christ (1Corinthians 12:13), God's *"chosen one"* (Luke 9:35; Isaiah 42:1), <u>after</u> they have chosen to repent and believe while depraved.

We must avoid confusing salvation with the blessings associated with salvation, a fact becoming increasingly obvious. Those who desire to equate know with choice or election fail to heed this warning, inundating their theology with contradiction to the confusion of many.

Note: Interestingly, "chosen," defined properly, could replace *"known"* in 1Corinthians 8:3 without violating the full counsel of God's Word. After all, "chosen" relates to the special office, or position, received by New Testament believers in conjunction with their being placed in Christ subsequent to exercising repentance and faith while depraved. "Chosen" does not, by any stretch of the imagination, point to the elect being elected (chosen) to salvation from eternity past by means of an eternal decree. This subject will be addressed in more detail when we study election as an independent topic.

Reformed Theology's View of *"Known"* in Galatians 4:8-9

Another New Testament verse cited by those who <u>attempt</u> to equate know with choice or election (in an effort to equate foreknow with foreordination or predestination) is Galatians 4:8-9.

> *8 However at that time, when you did not know God, you were*
> *slaves to those which by nature are no gods. 9 But now that you*
> *have come to know God, or rather to be <u>known by God</u>, how is it*
> *that you turn back again to the weak and worthless elemental*
> *things, to which you desire to be enslaved all over again?*
> (Galatians 4:8-9 NASB)

The phrase, *"known by God,"* does not mean chosen/elected by God in the sense of having been chosen/elected to salvation from eternity past, as many Calvinists believe. Yet Wayne Grudem (a Reformed theologian), tying his thoughts regarding Romans 8:29 to our present passages of interest (1Corinthians 8:3 and Galatians 4:9), in *BIBLE doctrine*, page 286, writes:

> Romans 8:29 can hardly be used to demonstrate that God based his
> predestination on foreknowledge of *the fact that a person would*
> *believe.* The passage speaks rather of the fact that God knew

> persons ("*those whom* He foreknew"), not that he knew some *fact about them*, such as the fact that they would believe. It is a personal, relational knowledge that is spoken of here: God, looking into the future, thought of certain people in saving relationship to himself, and in that sense he "knew them" long ago. This is the sense in which Paul can talk about God's "knowing" someone, for example, in 1 Corinthians 8:3: "But if one loves God, one is *known by him.*" Similarly, he says, "but now that you have come to know God, or rather *to be known by God...*" (Gal. 4:9). When people *know* God in Scripture, or when God *knows* them, it is personal knowledge that involves a saving relationship. Therefore, in Romans 8:29, "those whom he *foreknew*" is best understood to mean, "those whom he long ago *thought of in a saving relationship to himself*"....The text actually says nothing about God foreknowing or foreseeing that certain people would believe, nor is that idea mentioned in any other text of Scripture.[23]

Reformed Theology (extreme and hyper-Calvinism) cannot withstand the truth that God can know about future events without causing them. Neither can it withstand the truth that the word "*known*" in passages such as 1Corinthians 8:3 and Galatians 4:9 doesn't mean chosen or elected.

Forster and Marston, in *God's Strategy in Human History,* page 189, refute Grudem's previous conclusions:

> The line of argument seemingly used from it [Galatians 4:9] runs: "knowledge" in Galatians 4:9 means "election" or "marking out" and similarly "foreknowledge" means "chosen in advance." Yet the verse implies that their present state of knowing and being known by God has replaced a former state of non-knowledge. If God "fore-knew" them all along (in the supposed sense of election), how could Paul imply that the present state of mutual knowledge replaced a former state where neither "knew" the other?[24]

Forster and Marston's argument is more than valid, for Galatians 4:9 proves that a time existed when the Galatian believers did not know God and God did not know them. This period of "non-knowledge" occurred when they were unbelievers, and, therefore, not yet part of God's family. This fact is problematic for people who view foreknowledge as equivalent to foreordination or predestination. After all, had these believers been foreordained or predestined to salvation from eternity past by means of an eternal decree, they would have been known by God according to his view. Thus, this event sequence could not happen, for Paul teaches in

Galatians 4:8-9 that a time existed when they were <u>not</u> *"known by God."* Consequently, the verses used to make Reformed Theology's argument, negate Reformed Theology's argument. Again, we observe the confusion when *"known"* is equated with chosen in an attempt to redefine foreknowledge as foreordination or predestination.

What, then, is Galatians 4:8-9 communicating? Paul seems to be saying that the Galatians' former manner of life, consumed by idolatry, was greatly inferior to the life of faith. God's salvation, which is granted once the depraved repent and believe, allows New Testament believers not only to know God intimately (Philippians 3:10; Romans 8:15), but also to be known by Him in a way that supersedes anything imaginable. Just think, the God who spoke the world into existence views the souls and spirits of all members of Christ's body as *"holy"* (Ephesians 1:4), *"forgiven"* (Ephesians 4:32; Colossians 2:13; 1John 2:12), perfected (Hebrews 10:14), completed (Colossians 2:10), *"glorified"* (Romans 8:30), and much, much more. New Testament believers are placed in Christ as well as in the Father (John 14:10) and made *"new"* (2Corinthians 5:17), an event that transpires the moment they repent and believe while depraved. New Testament believers, as *"saints"* (1Corinthians 1:2), will, in addition, have the wonderful privilege of one day receiving their glorified bodies (Romans 8:23). Can we ever begin to imagine, having made us into all of the above and more, how deeply and intimately God knows us? Yes we, as church saints, are truly *"known by God"* (Galatians 4:8-9).

One more verse, Genesis 4:1, and we will move on.

Yada in Genesis 4:1

Individuals who redefine foreknow as foreordination or predestination attempt to link love with foreknew through the use of the Hebrew word *yada* in Genesis 4:1 which in this case is rendered *"knew"*:

> *And Adam knew [yada] Eve his wife* (Genesis 4:1, KJV)

Dave Hunt, in *What Love Is This?*, page 281, explains why Genesis 4:1 cannot be used to link *yada* (*"knew"*), and in turn foreknew, with loved beforehand:

> Other Calvinists point to the way sexual intercourse is expressed
> in the Old Testament: "Adam knew [*yada*] his wife" (Genesis 4:1),
> "Cain knew [*yada*] his wife" (verse 17), etc. They then suggest that
> "whom God foreknew" actually means "whom God loved
> beforehand." But that is nonsense.

> While *yada* is at times used to denote a special relationship—"I did know thee in the wilderness" (Hosea 13:5), "You only have I known of all the families of the earth" (Amos 3:2)—never does it mean to know in advance, whereas that is the principle meaning of *proginosko* and *prognosis*. There is, therefore, no relationship between these words that would be of any help in supporting Calvinism.
>
> Furthermore, to "know" one's wife in a sexual way could not be before the fact, nor does God "know" man in that manner. Therefore, the attempt to link love with foreknowledge through *yada*, to give the meaning "foreloved," won't work.[25]

Again, we see the contradictions that arise while attempting to redefine terms in God's inerrant Word.

Some Fair, Relevant Questions

Points previously addressed present enormous conflict for those who redefine foreknowledge as foreordination or predestination. Consider a few fair, relevant questions as a means to examine some of the challenges accompanying their thinking.

Incorrectly assume, for a moment at least, that foreknowledge means foreordination or predestination, and that God chose/elected the elect to salvation from eternity past by means of an eternal decree. This train of thought would imply more than God foreknowing the future. It would indicate that God acted in some way on those elected. Is God capable of action on human beings before they exist? Is it not at conception that a human being becomes a human being? In other words, is it possible for God to develop a special relationship with a person before a person becomes a person? Or, does God enter into a special relationship with an idea? How, however, can a cognizant being, God in this case, have a special relationship with an idea? He cannot! Therefore, God could not have elected the elect to salvation from eternity past (nor developed a special relationship with the elect before they exist). Yet, John MacArthur (a Reformed theologian) in *The MacArthur New Testament Commentary, Ephesians*, page 14, writes:

> Because in God's plan Christ was crucified for us "before the foundation of the world" (1 Pet. 1:20), we were designated for salvation by that same plan at that same time. It was then that our inheritance in God's kingdom was determined (Matt. 25:34). <u>We belonged to God before time began</u>, and we will be His after time has long run its course....[26]

Wow! Just think of the numerous contradictions included in these statements. Do you agree with the idea that you "belonged to God before time began"? The following refutes such thinking.

*D*oes God develop a special relationship with a person *before* a person becomes a person?

According to Ephesians 2:3, all persons are born spiritually dead to God, separated from God. This separation presents a gigantic problem for the theory that God chose/elected believers to salvation from eternity past by means of an eternal decree and, at the same time, entered into a special relationship with them. Such an arrangement would indicate that those chosen/elected to salvation, long before they are born, somehow lose their special relationship with God through conception and birth. Again we observe that contradiction reigns within Reformed Theology!

Time has arrived to transition into the New Testament verses that make use of terms such as *"foreknow," "foreknew",* and *"foreknowledge."* Allowing the previous input to serve as a backdrop will make the following material extremely enlightening.

B.A.S.I.C. TRAINING

CHAPTER FIVE

FOREKNOWLEDGE IN THE NEW TESTAMENT

PROGINOSKO, FROM WHICH WE GET the term "foreknow," is used only five times in the New Testament: Acts 26:4-5; Romans 8:29; Romans 11:2; 1Peter 1:20; 2Peter 3:17. In addition, *prognosis* is interpreted *"foreknowledge"* in Acts 2:23 and 1Peter 1:2. We will observe each of these seven passages and discover their contribution to this vital theological matter.

Romans 8:29

> *For whom He foreknew, He also predestined to become conformed to the image of His Son, that He might be the first-born among many brethren;*

We have confirmed that *"foreknew"* (*proginosko*) means "to know in advance in the sense of foreseeing." Based on Romans 8:29, the predestination of a New Testament believer cannot occur in an environment void of foreknowledge. Because God's purposes (Ephesians 3:11; 2Timothy 1:9) and decrees (Jeremiah 5:22) are eternal, He could not have known them in advance (foreknown them). Had He known them in advance, eternity would have a starting point and by definition eternity cannot have a beginning. Correspondingly, a New Testament believer could not have been predestined to salvation by means of an eternal decree (long before physical birth) because in that scenario foreknowledge would have no room to precede the decree (note Diagram 2, "Why God's Foreknowledge Cannot Precede His Eternal Decrees"). New Testament believers are predestined to receive a glorified body once they are placed in Christ subsequent to repenting and believing while depraved (Ephesians 1:5; Romans 8:23). Review **The Simplicity of Predestination** in the **Introduction** for additional input.

Keep this truth in mind as we continue. Also note: Predestination will be examined as a separate topic after foreknowledge.

1Peter 1:1-2

> ...*who are chosen according to the <u>foreknowledge</u> of God the Father...*

The same principles apply here as in Romans 8:29. Just as foreknowledge must precede predestination, *"foreknowledge"* must precede the believer's chosenness (election) as well (reference Diagram 2). Thus, for New Testament believers to have been chosen to salvation from eternity past by means of an eternal decree is impossible. New Testament believers are chosen <u>to office</u> once they are placed in Christ, God's *"chosen one"* (Luke 9:35; Isaiah 42:1), after repenting and believing while depraved. We will give more attention to what 1Peter 1:1-2 teaches regarding the believer's chosenness (election) later in this series.

1Peter 1:18-20

> *18 knowing that you were not redeemed with perishable things like silver or gold from your futile way of life inherited from your forefathers, 19 but with precious blood, as of a lamb unblemished and spotless, the blood of Christ. 20 For He was <u>foreknown</u> before the foundation of the world, but has appeared in these last times for the sake of you*

Verse 20 has suffered greatly at the hands of Bible translators. Unfortunately, the King James Version and the New King James Version translate the word *"foreknown"* (*proginosko*—v.20) as "foreordained." Foreordained (or predestined) is from a totally different Greek word (*proorizo*), as confirmed by verses such as Acts 4:28 and 1Corinthians 2:7. Even the Revised Standard Version takes the liberty to interpret the Greek word *proginosko* (*"foreknown"*) as *"destined,"* adding more abuse to 1Peter 1:20. The proper term is *"foreknown,"* not destined, foreordained, or predestined.

Jesus, the eternal Son of the Father, was *"foreknown"* by the Father *"before the foundation of the world"* (before creation). Is this Peter's point here, or is there a deeper meaning attached to his words? The deciding factor is the context of Peter's statements. In verses 10-12 of this chapter, Peter speaks of the Old Testament believers' inquisitiveness regarding the *"salvation"* provided by the suffering Savior. Yes, Old Testament believers had access to the Scriptures which spoke of a Savior Who would die (Psalm 22; Isaiah 53; etc.). They also observed the sacrificial system associated with the Law, which was a picture of what Christ would accomplish through the cross (Hebrews 10:1).   Yet, compared to New Testament believers' knowledge regarding Christ's life, death, burial, resurrection, and ascension, the Old Testament believers' knowledge was limited. The Father's foreknowledge, revealed in the Old Testament Scriptures, at least made them aware of Jesus' First Coming and corresponding crucifixion. For this knowledge they were extremely grateful, as is evidenced through the joy displayed by the Old Testament authors as they spoke of the coming Messiah.

With the above in mind, observe the phrase, *"For He was foreknown before the foundation of the world, but has appeared in these last times for the sake of you"* (1Peter 1:20). The context of this statement confirms that the Father, since before time began, has *"foreknown"* what Christ would accomplish through the cross—the actual event transpiring in time in 30 AD. Revelation 13:8 verifies the same truth.

However, Paul's words of Romans 3:25 bear witness to the fact that God *"passed over the sins"* of the Old Testament believers until Jesus could die on the cross. In other words, the Old Testament sacrifices only atoned for the believer's sins, never removing them, as also confirmed by Hebrews 9:1-10:12.

> *The Father foreknew what Christ would accomplish through the cross.*

Yet, these sacrifices served as a magnificent picture of what Christ would accomplish through His death, burial, resurrection, and ascension. No doubt, the word *"foreknown"* in 1Peter 1:20 points to the fact that the Father has known of the redemptive purpose, or function, of the eternal Son since before the world began, but did not allow this redemptive purpose, or function, to be fully manifested until the cross.

Calvin's View of 1Peter 1:18-20

Those theologians who redefine *"foreknown"* as foreordination or predestination approach 1Peter 1:20, as well as a wealth of additional verses, from a totally different perspective than has just been described.   In fact, they redefine *"foreknown"* hoping to prove that the elect were chosen (elected) to salvation from eternity past.   John Calvin, an advocate of this ideology, reveals where this misconception can lead. In fact, he concludes the unthinkable by seeming to deny Christ's eternal Sonship, oneness, and equality with the Father:

> It is wisely observed by Augustine, that in the very head of the
> Church we have a bright mirror of free election, lest it should give
> any trouble to us the members, viz., that he did not become the Son
> of God by living righteously, but was freely presented with this

> great honor, that he might afterwards make others partakers of his
> gifts. Should any one here ask, why others are not what he was, or
> why we are all at so great a distance from him, why we are all
> corrupt while he is purity, he would not only betray his madness,
> but his effrontery also. But if they are bent on depriving God of the
> free right of electing and reprobating, let them at the same time
> take away what has been given to Christ. (*Institutes*: Book 3;
> Chapter 22; Section 1—underline mine)[27]

Note that Calvin, by viewing *"foreknown"* (in verses such as 1Peter 1:20) as
foreordination or predestination, is free to incorrectly assume that Christ was
elected to Sonship:

> "...that in the very head of the Church we have a bright mirror of
> free election...." Book 3; Chapter 22; Section 1[28]

In the previous quote, Calvin also wrote:

> "that he did not become the Son of God by living righteously, but
> was freely presented with this great honor."[29]

The phrase, "did not become the Son of God by living righteously," has caused
some to view Psalm 2:7 as teaching that Jesus, instead of being the eternal Son of
God, became the Son of God:

> *"I will surely tell of the decree of the LORD: He said to Me, 'Thou
> art My Son, Today I have begotten Thee* (Psalm 2:7).

Can you believe what can result from redefining just one word, the word
"foreknown"? The subsequent rebuttal easily refutes this thinking.

Rebuttal to Calvin's View

The word, *"Today"* (Psalm 2:7), is extremely significant in that time began in
Genesis 1:1; time does not exist in eternity. Consequently, the phrase, *"Today
have begotten Thee,"* must point to an event that occurred in time, not from eternity
past. The word, *"begotten,"* is also important. Acts 13:33 proves that it points, not
to Jesus becoming the Son of God at some point in eternity past (Calvin's view)
but to His resurrection:

> *'That God has fulfilled this promise to our children in that He raised up Jesus, as it is also written in the second Psalm, 'THOU ART MY SON; TODAY I HAVE <u>BEGOTTEN</u> THEE'* (Acts 13:33)

Thus, if Jesus was the Son of God before His incarnation (Proverbs 30:4), how could He be anything but the eternal Son of God? Also, how could Jesus give anyone eternal life (John 10:28), life with no beginning and no end, if He is not the eternal Son, possessing such life Himself?

> *and I give eternal life to them, and they shall never perish; and no one shall snatch them out of My hand. (John 10:28)*

Romans 6:23 verifies the same truth:

> *For the wages of sin is death, but the free gift of God is eternal life in Christ Jesus our Lord.* (Romans 6:23)

Note that *"eternal life"* is found *"in Christ,"* which again confirms that Jesus is the eternal Son. And finally, Hebrews 1:8 removes all doubt:

> *But unto the Son he saith, Thy throne, O God, is for ever and ever: a scepter of righteousness is the scepter of thy kingdom.* (Hebrews 1:8 KJV)

How could Jesus be *"God"* without possessing life with no beginning and no end? It would be utterly impossible!

Again, we see the danger in redefining the word foreknown as foreordination or predestination. The bottom button associated with such thinking is nonsensical. Many strange doctrines, in addition to the one addressed here, have been generated as a result of this fatal error.

Conclusion: *"Foreknown,"* in 1Peter 1:20, means "to know beforehand." It cannot be redefined as foreordination, predestination, or predestined without interjecting a stockpile of error into one's perception of the Creator.

Acts 26:4-5

> *4 "So then, all Jews know my manner of life from my youth up, which from the beginning was spent among my own nation and at Jerusalem; 5 since they <u>have known</u> about me for a long time previously, if they are willing to*

> *testify, that I lived as a Pharisee according to the strictest sect of our religion.*

These verses confirm that *proginosko* (foreknow) can mean knowing about a person without establishing a special relationship with that person. This truth is important for future reference. Note how it applies to our present study of Acts 26:4-5.

Scripture verifies that Paul was well known among the Jews at Jerusalem. Therefore, as Paul addressed King Agrippa in Acts 26, he made reference to this fact. After all, he had studied under Gamaliel (Acts 22:3), a teacher of the Law (Acts 5:34) in Jerusalem, and had spent much time there serving as a devout follower of the Jewish traditions. Nonetheless, having been born in Tarsus (Acts 9:11; 21:39; 22:3), it is doubtful that every person in Jerusalem would have known him personally. Neither would they have had a close relationship with him. They did, however, know that he *"lived as a Pharisee according to the strictest sect of...* [his] *religion"* (Acts 26:5). One can only conclude, therefore, that *proginosko* in this case means a general knowledge of Paul. Thus, *proginosko* can mean knowing about a person without establishing a special relationship with that person. This fact proves that God can foreknow the thoughts, actions, decisions, works, etc. of an individual or group of individuals without a special relationship being involved.

Could this mean that God can foreknow the decisions of man without foreordaining (predestining) them from eternity past by means of an eternal decree, even the decisions the depraved exercise in choosing to repent and believe? You bet, as will continue to be verified as we proceed.

Romans 11:2

> *God has not rejected His people whom He foreknew.*

This verse points to God's foreknowledge of the Jewish people. But in what sense does foreknowledge apply to the context of Romans 11:2? It can apply in the following ways, but more than one reading may be necessary to fully comprehend the point being communicated.

1. God knows (foreknows) the thoughts, actions, decisions, and works of the Jewish people, just as with all mankind. The Jews, therefore, have never done anything that He did not know before the fact, including their disobedience. Thus, one application of *"foreknew"* (Romans 11:2), as it relates to the Jewish people, is God's pre-knowledge of their thoughts

actions, decisions, and works. This instance is very similar to what we addressed regarding Acts 26:4-5. There, we found that *proginosko* can mean knowing about a person without establishing a special relationship with that person. The same meaning applies in Romans 11:2 to God's foreknowledge of the thoughts, actions, decisions, and works of the Hebrew people. Of course, He did establish a special relationship with the Jews, as is indicated by (2), the next scenario, but in this instance (1), *"foreknew"* can point simply to God's pre-knowledge of Israel's thoughts, actions, decisions, and works.

2. Another application of *"foreknew,"* as it relates to the Jewish people, is God's special relationship with the nation. God entered into covenant, a special relationship, with the Hebrew people, understanding full well (foreknowing) that they would disobey. Even with all of this prior knowledge, He still established the following unconditional covenants with physical Israel:

    (a) The Abrahamic Covenant of Genesis 12:1-3

    (b) The Palestinian Covenant of Deuteronomy 30:1-10

    (c) The Davidic Covenant of 2Samuel 7:11b-16 and 1Chronicles 17:10-14

    (d) The New Covenant of Jeremiah 31:31-34

God also granted the Jews the privilege of receiving the Law (Exodus 20:1-17). He even married the nation soon afterwards in Exodus 24:1-8, paving the way for Jesus to be born a Jew.

God established a very special relationship with the Hebrew people. He chose them (Deuteronomy 7:6; 14:2) not only to be His wife, but also as *"a kingdom of priests"* (Exodus 19:6). As a kingdom of priests they were to take the good news of the coming Messiah to the Gentiles—something they have failed to do. But the Messiah was born a Jew, descendant of Abraham (Matthew 1:1), even though the Hebrew people failed to evangelize the Gentiles. Thus, the fact that God established a special relationship with the Jews is undeniable, a relationship rivaled by no other nation. After all, He married Israel! Consequently, the use of *"foreknew"* (Romans 11:2) possibly points to the special relationship that God established with the Jewish people.

Some theologians have taken this truth and attempted to prove that foreknowledge can be redefined as foreordination or predestination. We discovered the impossibility of such a scenario earlier in this study.

2Peter 3:17

> *You therefore, beloved, <u>knowing this beforehand</u>, be on your guard lest, being carried away by the error of unprincipled men, you fall from your own steadfastness,*

The meaning of the phrase, *"knowing this beforehand"* (*proginosko*), points to the knowledge of upcoming events. The upcoming events, in the context addressed by Peter, were associated with the false teachers who would attempt to distort the truth of the gospel.

Acts 2:23

> *this Man* [Jesus], *delivered up by the predetermined plan and <u>foreknowledge</u> of God, you nailed to a cross by the hands of godless men and put Him to death.*

Because God knows in advance (foreknows, from eternity past) the actions and hearts of all men, God's plans surrounding the cross could be accomplished without removing the free will of man. How could this feat come about? To bring about His will, God did not program the Jewish and Roman officials, nor those under their authority, to force them to crucify Jesus. Rather, knowing their hearts, He placed them in positions of leadership (Romans 13:1), understanding beforehand the choices they would make while serving in those positions. This placement allowed their unwise schemes to fulfill what God had planned regarding Jesus' trial and crucifixion. Consequently, those who had Jesus crucified *"fulfilled"* the Father's original plan (Acts 13:27) without being programmed to do so.

> *"For those who live in Jerusalem, and their rulers, recognizing neither Him nor the utterances of the prophets which are read every Sabbath, fulfilled these by condemning Him.* (Acts 13:27)

Based on Acts 13:27, Paul condemned those who failed to recognize Jesus. If the Father, by means of an eternal decree, caused them to respond in this manner yet condemned them for their actions, He would be anything but the just and loving God He claims to be in His inerrant letter to man.

The Error in the Opposing View

In Acts 2:23, Peter unmistakably distinguishes between *"predetermined plan"* (counsel, appointment, decree, etc.) and *"foreknowledge"* (*prognosis*—from the Greek root *proginosko*). *"Foreknowledge"* means "to know beforehand in the sense of foreseeing." *"Foreknowledge,"* therefore, is not equivalent to God's *"predetermined plan."* Should *"foreknowledge"* mean foreordination or predestination, Acts 2:23 would be unacceptably redundant by stating, "delivered up by the predetermined plan and predetermined plan of God," or "delivered up by the foreknowledge and foreknowledge of God." Such repetitiveness would be irrational. But, from our previous examination of Romans 11:2 and additional passages, we can understand how these individuals arrive at their incorrect conclusion. They begin with the Hebrew word *yada,* meaning "know," and attempt to make it mean choice. They then take the Greek word *ginosko,* meaning "know," the Greek equivalent of the Hebrew *yada,* and attempt to make it mean choice. If this alteration is possible (which it is not), they can then view *proginosko,* meaning foreknow, as meaning "to choose beforehand," and equate it with foreordination or predestination. This unsound reasoning, adopted by John MacArthur, caused him to write the following in *Saved Without A Doubt* (page 59):

> God's foreknowledge, therefore, is not a reference to His omniscient foresight but to His foreordination. God does indeed foresee who is going to be a believer, but the faith He foresees is the faith He Himself creates. It's not that He merely sees what will happen in the future; rather He ordains it. The Bible clearly teaches that God sovereignly chooses people to believe in Him.[30]

Because Paul makes a clear distinction between foreknowledge and foreordination (or predestination) in Romans 8:29, MacArthur's conclusions are incorrect:

> For whom He foreknew, He also [kai] predestined to become conformed to the image of His Son, (Romans 8:29, NASB)

Note Dave Hunt's quote from *What Love Is This?,* page 280, regarding the words, *"He also"* (Romans 8:29), from the Greek *kai:*

> The Greek *kai* denotes a differentiation, thus making it clear that foreknowledge could not be the same as predestination, or Paul…would be redundantly saying, "whom he did predestinate he also did predestinate.[31]

If *"foreknew"* meant predestined, the statement, "For whom He predestined, He also predestined," would be less than rational. Neither would, "For whom He foreknew, He also foreknew," make sense. Would Paul repeat himself for the sake of being redundant while addressing such an important matter? I think not! By making this statement, Paul confirms that *"foreknew"* and predestined are not equivalent.

Neither is foreknowledge the same as election or the believer's chosenness, as confirmed by 1Peter 1:1-2 (note that I have underlined *"foreknowledge," "Elect,"* and *"chosen"* in the following passages):

> *Peter, an apostle of Jesus Christ, to the strangers scattered*
> *throughout Pontus, Galatia, Cappadocia, Asia, and Bithynia, Elect*
> *according to the foreknowledge of God the Father, through*
> *sanctification of the Spirit, unto obedience and sprinkling of the*
> *blood of Jesus Christ: Grace unto you, and peace, be multiplied.*
> (1Peter 1:1-2 KJV)

> *Peter, an apostle of Jesus Christ, to those who reside as aliens,*
> *scattered throughout Pontus, Galatia, Cappadocia, Asia, and*
> *Bithynia, who are chosen according to the foreknowledge of God*
> *the Father, by the sanctifying work of the Spirit, that you may obey*
> *Jesus Christ and be sprinkled with His blood: May grace and*
> *peace be yours in fullest measure.* (1Peter 1:1-2 NASB)

Interestingly, John Piper (*Piper and Staff "Tulip,"* 22) contradicts these verses:

‖ foreknowledge is virtually the same as election[32]

The danger in redefining *"foreknowledge"* as foreordination or predestination i that the new definition requires that a series of resulting contradictions be classifie as mystery. The truth, however, is that God is not a God of contradiction. Even so some people argue that *"foreknew"* in Romans 8:29 cannot mean "to know i advance" because that definition would communicate that God could foreknow th thoughts, hearts, actions, and choices of believers only. Such statements are mad without taking into consideration the context of Romans 8:29:

> *For whom He foreknew, He also predestined...* (Romans 8:29—
> NASB)

Beginning with Romans 8:12 and continuing through Romans 8:28, Paul dea with truth pertaining to New Testament believers. The same context applies i

Romans 8:30-39. Consequently, Paul's reference to God's foreknowledge of the thoughts, hearts, actions, and choices of believers in Romans 8:29 in no way means that He does not also foreknow the thoughts, hearts, actions, and choices of unbelievers. God knows in advance all things that occur from eternity past through eternity future, including the thoughts, hearts, actions, and choices of believers and unbelievers alike. *"Cyrus,"* a Persian king who did not know Jehovah, confirms this fact (read Isaiah 45:1-4 with a special emphasis on verse 4). Therefore, God is not required to cause all things to know all things, as those who equate foreknowledge with foreordination and predestination many times assume. We will cover this subject in more detail when we address the free will of man as an independent topic.

SUMMARY OF TRUTHS LEARNED REGARDING GOD'S FOREKNOWLEDGE

Foreknowledge means "to know beforehand in the sense of foreseeing." It does not mean to foreordain or predestine. Consequently, foreknowledge cannot mean to choose beforehand. Because foreknowledge must precede the predestination (Romans 8:29) and election (1Peter 1:1-2) of New Testament believers, God could not have predestined or elected us to salvation from eternity past by means of an eternal decree. Eternity would have a beginning if such were true

F oreknowledge cannot precede an eternal decree. That would require eternity to have a beginning.

(review Diagrams 2 and 7 in the Reference Section). Thus, foreknowledge must point to God's ability to know beforehand the thoughts, hearts, actions, and choices of all mankind, in fact, everything that transpires. This definition not only confirms the free will of man, but also verifies that predestination must point to the glorious future destiny that God grants to New Testament believers once they are placed in Christ—subsequent to their repenting and believing while depraved. Thus, predestination, by no stretch of the imagination, points to God having predetermined man's destiny from eternity past by means of an eternal decree. This fact also confirms that election, or the believer's chosenness, must point to the special office, or position, that God grants to all church saints once they are placed in Christ after having exercised repentance and faith while depraved. John Calvin and Martin Luther, along with the entire community of Calvinists (including Reformed theologians), failed to consider this truth due to confusing the blessings associated with salvation with salvation itself. James Arminius was guilty of the same error. The in-depth, independent studies of predestination and election, which follow in this series, will support and expand these truths.

In closing, consider a quote from Charles Haddon Spurgeon (1834-1892), a very influential evangelist who is known as the "Prince of Preachers." He was a Calvinist, but as an evangelist struggled with some of the extreme views of Calvinism. Note what he states regarding these extreme views:

> "I cannot imagine a more ready instrument in the hands of Satan
> for the ruin of souls than a minister who tells sinners that it is not
> their duty to repent of their sins or to believe in Christ, and who has
> the arrogance to call himself a gospel minister, while he teaches
> that God hates some men infinitely and unchangeably for no reason
> whatever but simply because he chooses to do so." [*New Park
> Street Pulpit* (London: Passmore and Alabaster), Vol. 6, 28-29;
> sermon preached December 11, 1859]—quote taken from Dave
> Hunt's work, *What Love Is This?*, page 299.[33]

What is the origin of this error within Calvinism that Spurgeon, even though a Calvinist, so vehemently opposed? It began, not with the disciples or early church fathers, but with Augustine (354-430 AD)—who initially believed in the free will of man (and that the depraved can exercise repentance and faith), but eventually rejected that belief, later teaching that God predetermined man's destiny from eternity past by means of an eternal decree because man lacks the ability to exercise repentance and faith while depraved. Foreknowledge then came to be viewed as foreordination or predestination. The following chart, taken from Dr. Norm Geisler's, *Systematic Theology, Volume Three, Sin Salvation*, page 381, illustrates Augustine's radical theological shift:

Early Augustine	Later Augustine
God wills all to be saved	God wills only some to be saved
God never compels free will	God compels free will
God loves all	God loves only some
Saving faith is not a special gift to some	Saving faith is a special gift to only some
Fallen people can receive salvation	Fallen people cannot receive salvation[34]

No wonder Calvin, so highly influenced by Augustine, wrote the following:

> We say, then, that Scripture clearly proves this much, that God by his <u>eternal and immutable counsel</u> determined once for all those whom it was his pleasure one day to admit to salvation, and those whom, on the other hand, it was his pleasure to doom to destruction. We maintain that this counsel, as regards the elect, is founded on his free mercy, without any respect to human worth, while those whom he dooms to destruction are excluded from access to life by a just and blameless, but at the same time incomprehensible judgment. In regard to the elect, we regard calling as the evidence of election, and justification as another symbol of its manifestation, until it is fully accomplished by the attainment of glory. But as the Lord seals his elect by calling and justification, so by excluding the reprobate either from the knowledge of his name or the sanctification of his Spirit, he by these marks in a manner discloses the judgment which awaits them. (*Institutes*: Book 3; Chapter 21; Section 7)[35]

What is the moral to the story? Be sure to know the origin of what you believe. Truth alone, based on the full counsel of God's Word, is the only safeguard against the lies of the deceiver, Satan himself.

This concludes our study of foreknowledge. Allowing our discoveries to assist us in our in-depth study of predestination will be fascinating indeed. I trust you have been encouraged.

PART FOUR ❧ CHAPTER SIX

PREDESTINATION

PREDESTINATION BECOMES VERY SIMPLE when addressed in the light of our previous study of foreknowledge, so enjoy what the Scriptures record regarding this captivating subject. For a quick review, you can reference **The Simplicity of Predestination** in the **Introduction**.

Predestined...to Adoption as Sons

According to Ephesians 1:5, God predestines New Testament believers *"to adoption as sons"*:

> He *predestined us to adoption as sons* through Jesus Christ to Himself, according to the kind intention of His will, (Ephesians 1:5)

Note the word *"us"* in this passage. As a result of Paul's use of this term, and considering that Paul was a believer while writing to church saints at Ephesus, is it any wonder that the full counsel of God's Word teaches that only believers, who are already believers, are predestined? Nowhere in the Scriptures do we find that potential believers have been predestined from eternity past, as some people have incorrectly assumed. Therefore, New Testament believers are not predestined until God makes them new—subsequent to their exercising repentance and faith while depraved. How can we be certain of this fact? The phrase, *"adoption as sons,"* according to Romans 8:23, points to that day when all church saints receive their resurrected bodies:

> *And not only this, but also we ourselves, having the first fruits of*
> *the Spirit, even we ourselves groan within ourselves, waiting*
> *eagerly for <u>our adoption as sons, the redemption of our body</u>.*
> (Romans 8:23)

Linking the phrase, *"our adoption as sons, the redemption of our body"* (Romans 8:23), to the phrase, *"predestined us to adoption as sons"* (Ephesians 1:5), we can conclude the following:

A New Testament believer is *"predestined"* to receive a glorified *"body"* once he/she is placed in Christ and made new—<u>after</u> having exercised personal repentance and faith while depraved.

Yes, we were *"predestined"* to one day receive resurrected bodies. We were given this glorious future destiny once we were placed in Christ through the Person of the *"Spirit"* (1Corinthians 12:13) and made *"new"* (2Corinthians 5:17)—subsequent to our exercising personal repentance and faith while depraved. Clearly, the predestination of New Testament believers occurs in time, not from eternity past. We were *"predestined"* in time to blessings associated with salvation, not *"predestined"* from eternity past to one day be saved from the penalty of sin. (Reference Diagram 8, "Scriptural Election/Chosenness and Predestination.")

Simple! Nothing to it! Teachings about predestination which are contrary to this full counsel view are responsible for the confusion. Realize that Ephesians 1:5 and Romans 8:23 will be addressed in greater depth shortly.

Note: A New Testament believer is a believer who lives during the church age, an age which began in Acts 2 and will continue through the Rapture of the church.

Studying this subject matter is exciting, for it will greatly enhance our perception of Who God is. It will also equip us to defend what we believe regarding this incredibly important theological matter. Our understanding of foreknowledge should be enhanced as well.

The Six Mentions of *"Predestined"* in God's Word

Interestingly, the word predestination is not found in God's Word. However, *proorizo*, from which we get *"predestined,"* is used six times: Acts 4:28; Romans 8:29; Romans 8:30; 1Corinthians 2:7; Ephesians 1:5; Ephesians 1:11. Only Romans 8:29, Romans 8:30, Ephesians 1:5, and Ephesians 1:11 give input pertaining to how the New Testament believer is *"predestined."*

Our Approach to Predestination

We will begin by studying the six verses that contain *"predestined"* and interpret the context of *proorizo* (*"predestined"*) within each.   We will follow with Calvinism and Arminianism's teachings concerning the subject.   We will also address the origin of their views and explore Calvinism's TULIP.   After examining how Arminianism differs with the TULIP, we will finish with a summary of what we have discovered regarding the term *"predestined."*

The Outline of our Study

I.   The Contextual View Of *"Predestined"* (Acts 4:28; 1Corinthians 2:7; Romans 8:29; Romans 8:30; Ephesians 1:5; Ephesians 1:11)

II.   The Awesomeness of *"According To"*

III.   The Opposing Views, And How They Came Into Existence

IV.   The TULIP: Hyper, Extreme, And Moderate Calvinism's General Views

V.   How Arminianism Generally Views The TULIP

VI.   A Summary Of Discoveries Regarding The Term *"Predestined"*

CHAPTER SEVEN

I. THE CONTEXTUAL VIEW OF *"PREDESTINED'*

"Predestined" in Acts 4:28, the Contextual View

> *to do whatever Thy hand and Thy purpose <u>predestined</u> to occur.* (Acts 4:28)

BEFORE CONTINUING, you should take time to read Acts 4:23-31.

To bring about His *"purpose,"* God did not program the Jewish and Roman officials, nor those under their authority, in order to force them to crucify Jesus. Rather, knowing their hearts, He placed them in positions of leadership (Romans 13:1), understanding beforehand the choices they would make while serving in these positions. This placement allowed their unwise schemes to fulfill what God had *"predestined to occur"* regarding Jesus' trial and crucifixion, as confirmed by Acts 4:25:

> *"Why did the Gentiles rage, and the peoples devise futile things?"*
> (Acts 4:25)

The word *"devise"* (Acts 4:25) is from the same root word (*meletao*) that is rendered *"Take pains"* (NASB), or *"Meditate"* (KJV) in 1Timothy 4:15, words relating to man's ability to make his own choices. Consequently, the men who grossly mistreated Jesus during His rejection, trial, and crucifixion, determined for themselves the choices they would make. Their response, most definitely, was <u>not</u> due to God's programming, a fact also confirmed by Acts 13:27:

> *"For those who live in Jerusalem, and their rulers, recognizing*
> *neither Him nor the utterances of the prophets which are read*
> *every Sabbath, fulfilled these by condemning Him.* (Acts 13:27)

Should the Father have caused these Jews (referenced in Acts 13:27) to grossly mistreat Jesus, He would be totally unjust in bringing judgment against their actions because they (in such a scenario) would be judged for what had been impossible to avoid.

Conclusion: God *"predestined"* that Jesus would be crucified, a fact also validated by Luke 22:22. He did not predestine the behavior of the men responsible for His crucifixion. (Reference Diagram 9 before continuing.)

"Predestined" in 1Corinthians 2:7, the Contextual View

> *but we speak God's wisdom in a mystery, the hidden wisdom, which*
> *God predestined before the ages to our glory;* (1Corinthians 2:7)

When 1Corinthians 2:7 is studied in the context of 1Corinthians 2:6-16, one learns that the *"hidden wisdom"* that God has *"predestined"* is the *"wisdom"* revealed to the mature New Testament believer. This *"wisdom"* is not granted to believers possessing little interest in spiritual growth. Nor is it granted to Reformed Theology's "elect," who, according their view, are spiritually regenerated prior to believing, receiving this *"hidden wisdom"* in association with their spiritual regeneration. (Note: Reformed Theology is extreme and hyper-Calvinism. For more input, study Diagrams 10 and 11 in the Reference Section.)

Let's read 1Corinthians 2:6-16:

> *6 Yet we do speak wisdom among those who are mature; a wisdom,*
> *however, not of this age, nor of the rulers of this age, who are*
> *passing away; 7 but we speak God's wisdom in a mystery, the*
> *hidden wisdom, which God predestined before the ages to our*
> *glory; 8 the wisdom which none of the rulers of this age has*
> *understood; for if they had understood it, they would not have*
> *crucified the Lord of glory; 9 but just as it is written, "Things*
> *which eye has not seen and ear has not heard, And which have not*
> *entered the heart of man, All that God has prepared for those who*
> *love Him." 10 For to us God revealed them through the Spirit; for*
> *the Spirit searches all things, even the depths of God. 11 For who*
> *among men knows the thoughts of a man except the spirit of the*
> *man, which is in him? Even so the thoughts of God no one knows*

> *except the Spirit of God. 12 Now we have received, not the spirit of the world, but the Spirit who is from God, that we might know the things freely given to us by God, 13 which things we also speak, not in words taught by human wisdom, but in those taught by the Spirit, combining spiritual thoughts with spiritual words. 14 But a natural man does not accept the things of the Spirit of God; for they are foolishness to him, and he cannot understand them, because they are spiritually appraised. 15 But he who is spiritual appraises all things, yet he himself is appraised by no man. 16 For who has known the mind of the Lord, that he should instruct Him? But we have the mind of Christ. (1Corinthians 2:6-16)*

The phrase, *"Yet we do speak wisdom among those who are mature;..."* (v.6), confirms that this *"predestined"* *"wisdom"* (vv.6-7) is revealed to the *"mature"* church saint only—not to the lost (vv.8-10). Paul then describes the advantage that a mature New Testament believer has over the *"natural man,"* or unspiritual man (vv.11-16). The verses that follow (1Corinthians 3:1-3), which state that Paul fed these saints with *"milk"* instead of the *"solid food"* of the Word (due to their lack of maturity), confirm our conclusions:

> *1 And I, brethren, could not speak to you as to spiritual men, but as to men of flesh, as to babes in Christ. 2 I gave you milk to drink, not solid food; for you were not yet able to receive it. Indeed, even now you are not yet able, 3 for you are still fleshly. For since there is jealousy and strife among you, are you not fleshly, and are you not walking like mere men?* (1Corinthians 3:1-3)

Hebrews 5:13-14 verifies the same principle:
> *13 For everyone who partakes only of milk is not accustomed to the word of righteousness, for he is a babe. 14 But solid food is for the mature, who because of practice have their senses trained to discern good and evil.* (Hebrews 5:13-14)

Conclusion: The *"hidden wisdom"* that is *"predestined"* (1Corinthians 2:7) is the *"wisdom"* granted to the mature New Testament believer. Consequently, 1Corinthians 2:7 cannot be used to support the Reformed view—that man is born so totally depraved that God must spiritually regenerate the elect and grant them this hidden wisdom <u>before</u> they can choose to repent, believe, and be saved (reference Diagrams 10 and 11). Dave Hunt, in *What Love Is This?*, page 119, agrees:

81

> The Calvinist uses this passage [1Corinthians 2:7] to support the idea of "total depravity"—i.e., that only the elect who have been regenerated can understand and believe the gospel. Paul, however, is here speaking of more than the simple gospel; he is referring to the deeper understanding of spiritual truth that comes with maturity in Christ.[36]

We are confirming, over and over again, the value of the contextual view of the Scriptures. Isn't this exciting?! (Review Diagram 9 before continuing).

"Predestined" in Romans 8:29, the Contextual View

For whom He foreknew, He also <u>predestined</u> to become conformed to the image of His Son, that He might be the first-born among many brethren; (Romans 8:29)

(Be sure to make use of the diagrams included in the Reference Section. They will serve you well as we proceed. Also, keep in mind that Paul is describing how predestination relates to New Testament believers—not believers plus potential believers.)

Note the Transition

The use of *"predestined"* in Acts 4:28 and 1 Corinthians 2:7 does <u>not</u> relate to the New Testament believer's destiny. Romans 8:29 is the first of the four remaining verses containing the word, *"predestined,"* that does. The other three verses (Romans 8:30; Ephesians 1:5; Ephesians 1:11) also relate to the destiny of New Testament believers and will be addressed shortly.

The Application of Foreknowledge

We have learned that foreknowledge must precede the predestination of church saints. However, foreknowledge is not required to precede the predestination addressed in Acts 4:28 (relating to Christ's crucifixion) and 1Corinthians 2:7 (relating to the *"hidden wisdom"* granted to the mature New Testament believer). God's decrees as well as His foreknowledge are eternal. Therefore, God, by means of an eternal decree, <u>can</u> predestine the crucifixion of Christ (Acts 4:28) as well as the *"hidden wisdom"* (1Corinthians 2:7) without contradiction. These events are

82

not according to His foreknowledge, unlike the predestination of the New Testament believer, which is. Consequently, God's foreknowledge must precede the predestination of the New Testament believer. Foreknowledge is not required to precede the predestination mentioned in Acts 4:28 and 1Corinthians 2:7. Reference Diagrams 2 and 9 for further input.

Before we address the word *"predestined"* as it relates to Romans 8:29, we need to quickly review what we know regarding the word *"foreknew."*

God possesses foreknowledge, which means "to know in advance in the sense of foreseeing." Thus, God's foreknowledge has allowed Him to know in advance (foreknow) everything that man has chosen in the past. God also knows in advance (foreknows) what man will choose in the future, even throughout eternity. Yes, God has given man a free will. Yet, God knows beforehand what man's choices will be (Psalm 139:1-4).

Note: When Psalm 139:1-16 is studied closely, one learns that, besides knowing the actions, thoughts, and words of David, God knew David himself, David the person. In fact, God knew David from the time of his conception in his mother's womb (verses 13-16)—in the same way that He knew Jeremiah in Jeremiah 1:5. Psalm 139:1-16 does not teach that God's foreknowledge of David caused David to act as he acted.

Based on Romans 8:29, God's foreknowledge, meaning "to know beforehand in the sense of foreseeing," must precede the predestination of a New Testament believer:

"For whom He foreknew, He also predestined..." (Romans 8:29)

Foreknowledge cannot precede predestination if believers were predestined to salvation from eternity past by means of an eternal decree (Arminianism and Calvinism's view). Why? Nothing, not even God's foreknowledge, can precede His eternal decrees. Because God's eternal decrees have always existed within His heart, nothing can precede them. (Diagram 2 in the Reference Section displays this fact in graphic form.) Consequently, the idea that the elect were predestined to salvation from eternity past by means of an eternal decree is incorrect. When, then, is a New Testament believer predestined—and to what is he/she predestined? A New Testament believer is predestined (once he/she becomes a new creation through being placed in Christ by means of the Holy Spirit, subsequent to repenting and believing while depraved) to receive a glorified body, a body to be obtained at the Rapture of the church. In this case, ample room is available for God's foreknowledge to precede predestination, as is required by Romans 8:29.

The Specifics of New Testament Believers' Predestination

Since New Testament believers are not predestined to salvation, to what, then, are they predestined? They are predestined to blessings associated with the salvation granted by God to those who choose, while depraved, to repent and believe. Thus, they are predestined to blessings in conjunction with being placed in Christ after repenting and believing while depraved. They most definitely were not predestined to salvation from eternity past by means of an eternal decree, as the Calvinists and Arminians believe (see Diagrams 4-7).

Romans 8:29 confirms that God possesses foreknowledge—the ability to know in advance. However, the fact that God has foreknowledge does not mean that He has eliminated man's ability to make his own choices. All persons have a free will and can choose, while depraved, whether they will accept or reject Christ. Consequently, we were not predestined from eternity past, nor were we predestined to become believers. Rather, in conjunction with being placed in Christ, subsequent to repenting and believing while depraved, we were given a glorious future destiny—that of receiving a glorified body at the Rapture of the church. As a result, New Testament believers have been granted a destiny: to be *"conformed to the image of His* [the Father's] *Son"* (Romans 8:29)—Who now possesses a resurrected body like the body we will receive at the Rapture. Thus, only believers are predestined—after they exercise personal repentance and faith while depraved.

Clearly, New Testament believers are predestined when they are placed in Christ and made new (2Corinthians 5:17), after repenting and believing while depraved. Proper interpretation of the intriguing phrase, *"that He might be the first-born among many brethren"* (Romans 8:29), however, requires noting its relationship to the previous phrases in the passage:

> *For whom He foreknew, He also predestined to become conformed*
> *to the image of His Son, that He might be the first-born among*
> *many brethren;* (Romans 8:29)

Jesus is *"the first-born"* of the Father in the sense that He was the first to receive a resurrected body. Colossians 1:18 validates this fact:

> *...and He is the beginning, the first-born from the*
> *dead...*(Colossians 1:18)

If Jesus is described as *"the first-born"* of the Father due to His bodily resurrection (Colossians 1:18), then Romans 8:29 must point not only to Jesus' bodily resurrection, but also to the future bodily resurrection of all New Testament believers:

> *...that He might be the first-born among many brethren;* (Romans 8:29)

The fact that we are part of the "*many brethren*" confirms that God "*predestined*" us (after we exercised repentance and faith while depraved) to receive a glorified body at the Rapture of the church. Many blessings accompany this wonderful event. Consequently, church saints will live throughout the Millennium and the Eternal Order in a glorified body, responding properly to the variables placed before them. Why will this be the case? Each church saint will live in a body, not only void of the old brain, which houses sinful habit patterns (and godly habit patterns as well), but a body void of the power of sin, a power which lives in the body of every believer (and unbeliever as well) during his/her stay on the earth (Romans 7:23). (The *Romans 1-8* course distributed by this ministry addresses this subject in greater depth.) No doubt, the New Testament believer has been given a glorious future destiny—that of receiving a glorified body at the Rapture of the church.

This truth ties in perfectly with 1Corinthians 15:51-55:

> *...we shall not all sleep, but we shall all be changed, in a moment, in the twinkling of an eye, at the last trumpet; for the trumpet will sound, and the dead will be raised imperishable, and we shall be changed. For this perishable must put on the imperishable, and this mortal must put on immortality. But when this perishable will have put on the imperishable, and this mortal will have put on immortality, then will come about the saying that is written, "DEATH IS SWALLOWED UP in victory. "O DEATH, WHERE IS YOUR VICTORY? O DEATH, WHERE IS YOUR STING?"* (1Corinthians 15:51-55)

Be sure to realize that the resurrection addressed in 1Corinthians 15:51-55 is different from Lazarus' experience in John 11. Lazarus was raised back to natural life, back to mortal life, meaning that his body would die a second time. This same principle applies to all individuals raised back to natural life, such as Tabitha in Acts 9:36-43. Jesus' body, on the other hand, was resurrected to immortal life, never to die again. It was to this immortal life in the bodily sense (addressed in 1Corinthians 15:51-55) that we were predestined once we were placed in Christ (and given eternal life in soul and spirit) subsequent to repenting and believing while depraved.

Note: When a New Testament believer dies, his/her holy and blameless eternal soul and spirit eject out of the physical (mortal) body and instantaneously enter heaven (2Corinthians 5:8) while the physical (mortal) body returns to dust. At the Rapture, the church saint's holy and blameless eternal soul and spirit will be joined to his/her newly resurrected (immortal) body for all eternity (1Thessalonians 4:13-18).

Conclusion: Predestination has no relation to whether a person will or will not be saved/justified.   Scriptural predestination is easily understood and can be summed up as follows: All who accept Christ, while depraved, during the church age, are given a glorious future destiny in conjunction with being placed in Christ and made new. Because God possesses foreknowledge, He knows beforehand who will accept Him and receive this glorious future destiny. He also knows who will not. This truth will greatly simplify the three remaining verses where *"predestined"* is found. (For additional input, be sure to make use of the diagrams included in the Reference Section.)

"Predestined" in Romans 8:30, the Contextual View

> *and whom He <u>predestined</u>, these He also called; and whom He called, these He also justified; and whom He justified, these He also glorified.* (Romans 8:30)

Paul states that those whom God *"predestined,"* He also *"called"*—*"called"* in this case meaning to name or give a role (or position) within the body of Christ to New Testament believers once they are placed in Christ subsequent to repenting and believing while depraved (Romans 1:1: Ephesians 4:1).   (Based on 1Corinthians 1:9, *"called"* can also mean a general call *"into fellowship with"* the *"Lord,"* which does not seem to fit the context of Romans 8:30.) Continuing with Romans 8:30, God also justifies all who believe during the church age (to be *"justified"* means to have been made not guilty). He glorifies their souls and spirits at that time as well (v.30).

With the previous input in mind, it becomes apparent that God makes the souls and spirits of New Testament believers into a finished product at the point of salvation/justification. Yes, God has already *"glorified"* our souls and spirits if we have chosen to accept Christ, even though we continue to sin so long as we live in earthly bodies! The words *"predestined," "called," "justified,"* and *"glorified"* are all in the aorist tense, pointing to past action. Consequently, what Paul describes here is experienced the moment a person, during the church age, is placed in Christ subsequent to repenting and believing while depraved.

Not Chronological

Romans 8:30 does not, as some theologians have wrongly assumed, give the chronological order of events in the life of a believer. In other words, it does not teach that God first *"predestined"* us (from eternity past) to be saved, then *"called"* us when it was our time to be saved, then *"justified"* us, and will, in the future, glorify us. That sequence is impossible since all of these verbs are in the past tense. Thus, if we are believers, all of this action has already occurred. It took place the moment we exercised repentance and faith, while depraved, and were placed in Christ. Realize as well that God *"foreknew"* (Romans 8:29) that this action would occur. He *"foreknew"* that we would choose to believe and, thus, receive these blessings, without causing us to believe.

Amazingly, Arminianism and all forms of Calvinism perceive Romans 8:30 as teaching that all believers (past, present, and future) were predestined to salvation from eternity past by means of an eternal decree. However, this view would allow Romans 8:30 to teach that the *"predestined"* of Arminianism and Calvinism who are not yet in existence are presently *"called,"* *"justified,"* and *"glorified"*—since *"predestined,"* *"called,"* *"justified,"* and *"glorified"* are all in the past tense. Stated differently, had future believers been *"predestined"* to salvation from eternity past, they would presently be *"called,"* *"justified,"* and *"glorified."* This arrangement, however, would cause them to be *"justified"* and *"glorified"* prior to existing as well as *"justified"* and *"glorified"* at physical birth. Therefore, passages such as Ephesians 2:3 discredit both Arminianism and all forms of Calvinism (including Reformed Theology), for all persons arrive on the earth *"children of wrath."*

> *Among them we too all formerly lived in the lusts of our flesh,*
> *indulging the desires of the flesh and of the mind, and were by*
> *nature children of wrath, even as the rest.*   (Ephesians 2:3)

Note: The *Advancing in Romans 1-8* study (distributed by this ministry) addresses Romans 8:30 in much greater depth.

The Context of *"Glorified"*

You may ask, "Is it not when I *'see'* Christ that I will be glorified (1John 3:2)? Doesn't Philippians 3:21 teach that God *'will transform the body of our humble state into conformity with the body of His glory,'* and doesn't this transformation take place at some point after we are released from our earthly bodies?" No doubt, New Testament believers will receive their glorified bodies at some point in the future. In Romans 8:30, however, Paul refers not to the body but to the spirit and soul (to the new creation we became when we were placed in Christ). When we were placed in Christ (2Corinthians 5:17), and Christ came to live in us (Galatians 2:20), subsequent to our repenting and believing while depraved, we were born again (saved/justified)—at which time we received a glorified soul and spirit. This transformation occurred instantaneously! Nonetheless, we will continue to commit acts of sin so long as we live in earthly bodies. Yet, even then, we are glorified saints who have made temporary mistakes—not lowly, second-class citizens of the kingdom.

The Scriptural Distinction Between Predestination and Salvation (Justification)

In Romans 8:30, Paul makes a distinction between the New Testament believer's predestination and salvation (justification). Dave Hunt, in *What Love Is This?*, page 282, writes the following:

> ...not only is predestination/election never said to be unto
> salvation, but Paul [in Romans 8:30] carefully separates
> predestination from salvation, whether in its call, its justification,
> or its glorification... The Greek *kai* shows that a distinction is
> being made: predestination is not the same as calling, justification,
> or glorification.[37]

Justification (salvation) is not the same as predestination. Justification is the New Testament believer receiving a holy, perfect, and blameless soul and spirit through being placed in Christ, <u>after</u> repenting and believing while depraved. Predestination, on the other hand, relates to the glorious future destiny the New Testament believer receives through being placed in Christ <u>after</u> repenting and believing while depraved. While addressing Romans 8:29, we discussed that this glorious future destiny relates to several issues, the main of which is the glorified body the church saint receives at the Rapture of the church.

The additional input of Ephesians 1:5 and Ephesians 1:11 regarding the term *"predestined"* should be extremely stimulating.

"Predestined" in Ephesians 1:5, the Contextual View

> He <u>predestined</u> us to adoption as sons through Jesus Christ to
> *Himself, according to the kind intention of His will.* (Ephesians
> 1:5)

Comprehending the full impact of this passage is impossible unless we first study verses 1-4 of Ephesians 1. In fact, because the final verse that contains the word *"predestined"* is located in verse 11 of this same chapter, we will observe several verses in Ephesians 1 to make certain of the context of both passages.

(Note: The *Ephesians* course distributed by this ministry explains Ephesians 1 in much greater depth. What a remarkable chapter!)

> *Paul, an apostle of Christ Jesus by the will of God, to the saints*
> *who are at Ephesus, and who are faithful in Christ Jesus:*
> (Ephesians 1:1)

Paul addresses his apostolic authority in this passage as well as the fact that New Testament believers are *"saints"* (not lowly sinners) and *"faithful."*

> *Grace to you and peace from God our Father and the Lord Jesus*
> *Christ.* (Ephesians 1:2)

"Peace," which results from accepting God's *"grace"* in the midst of one's circumstances, is a *"fruit of the Spirit"* (Galatians 5:22). This verse confirms that the Godhead is the Source of all *"grace"* and *"peace."*

> *Blessed be the God and Father of our Lord Jesus Christ, who has*
> *blessed us with every spiritual blessing in the heavenly places in*
> *Christ,* (Ephesians 1:3)

As we continue, be aware that verses 3-14 comprise one sentence in the original Greek. Paul begins by blessing (praising) *"the God and Father of our Lord Jesus Christ,"* the Source of all blessings—including those listed in verses 3-14. Blessing, or praising God comes naturally once one has a proper view of His blessings. In fact, blessing, praise, and adoration are a natural byproduct of understanding the heart of God and His provision for man. Paul praised (blessed) God not only for the blessings he had received through Christ, but also because of his understanding of God's heart and His ultimate plan and purpose in the gospel. Let me explain.

Do you realize that God's idea of a good time is blessing His people? The moment we were saved (justified—Romans 5:1), God gave us everything needed to live life to the fullest. In fact, until our bodies cease to operate, we will be digging through that huge treasure chest of spiritual blessings we received the moment we accepted Christ and received God's salvation. For this reason, and a host of others, we should go on to spiritual maturity because only then can we begin to comprehend all that is already ours. Some individuals in the body of Christ, due to nominal hunger for truth, are "doing" to try to attain what is already theirs. This behavior results in nothing but defeat and despair—a big smile and very sad eyes.

God has blessed us with these spiritual blessings *"in the heavenly places in Christ"* (Ephesians 1:3b). Because Christ is now at the right hand of the Father (Hebrews 8:1-2; 9:24), to be placed into Christ means that we have been taken into the realm of the heavenlies. Thus, Paul's words are, *"who has blessed us with every spiritual blessing in the heavenly places in Christ"* (Ephesians 1:3b). In other words, when a person during the church age repents of sin and accepts Christ through faith (while depraved), he/she, through the avenue of the Holy Spirit (1Corinthians 12:13), is placed into Christ and made new (2Corinthians 5:17). I don't pretend to understand even a small portion of the positive ramifications here. But one point is certain: All who repent and believe (while depraved) during the church age are then placed *in Christ"* (2Corinthians 5:17), and all who are *"in Christ"* have been blessed *"with every spiritual blessing"* needed to live life abundantly (Ephesians 1:3b). So, if you are God's child, give up on trying to perform well enough to obtain more spiritual blessings. They are already yours. *"Rest,"* therefore, and enjoy the journey as we look at just a few of these extraordinary blessings (Hebrews 4:9-10)!

As we continue, take special note of the phrases *"in Christ"* and *"in Him."* Take these phrases out of the epistle to the Ephesians, and you have a different epistle. In fact, taking them out of the New Testament would result in utter chaos. However, beginning to view your walk from this perspective will result in the realization that whatever you are, or possess, is *"in Christ."*

The Scriptures also speak of Christ living in all church saints. Passages such as Galatians 2:20 and Colossians 1:27 confirm that Jesus most definitely lives in all (during the church age) who have accepted Him as Savior. But, the Scriptures speak much more about the New Testament believer being *"in Christ"* than they speak of Christ dwelling in the New Testament believer. Therefore, from what vantage point would the Lord have us live? From the heavenly vantage point, of course!

Take special note of the phrases "in Christ" and "in Him."

Paul next states:

> just as He <u>chose us in Him</u> before the foundation of the world, that
> we should be holy and blameless before Him. In love (Ephesians
> 1:4)

One of the many spiritual blessings received by believers during the church age is: The Father *"chose"* them in Christ *("in Him")* *"before the foundation of the world"* (Ephesians 1:4a). We must be careful here. Several strange doctrines have

90

evolved from an improper view of this passage.

Location of Church Saint's Chosenness

The fact that God chooses New Testament believers is a given. However, <u>where</u> He chooses them is of utmost importance if we are to properly interpret Paul's words. Notice that church saints are chosen in Christ ("*in Him*"—Ephesians 1:4a). Consequently, New Testament believers are not chosen to be placed into Christ, but rather are chosen once they are in Christ. Thus, New Testament believers are not chosen until they are in Christ. The Scriptures teach that they are not placed in Christ and made new creations until they have exercised personal repentance and faith while depraved (John 1:11-12; Acts 16:31; Acts 26:18; 2Corinthians 5:17). As a result, *"chose us in Him"* (Ephesians 1:4) cannot point to the false idea that the elect were chosen to salvation from eternity past by means of an eternal decree—Arminianism and Calvinism's view.

The Mechanics of Church Saints' Chosenness

We must understand that being placed in Christ through the power of the Holy Spirit (1Corinthians 12:13), subsequent to exercising repentance and faith while depraved, is what allows the New Testament believer to be chosen and, therefore, share in Christ's chosenness. The following input explains in more depth how this becomes a reality.

Christ, according to Luke 9:35, was chosen:

> *"This is My Son, <u>My Chosen One</u>; listen to Him!"* (Luke 9:35)

Isaiah 42:1 also speaks of Christ's chosenness:

> *"Behold, My Servant, whom I uphold; <u>My chosen one</u> in whom My soul delights. I have put My Spirit upon Him; He will bring forth justice to the nations."* (Isaiah 42:1)

God the Father chose Jesus to be the Savior of the world, which is further confirmed in Luke 23:35, 1Peter 2:4, and 1Peter 2:6:

> *And the people stood by, looking on. And even the rulers were sneering at Him, saying, "He saved others; let Him save Himself if this is the Christ of God, His <u>Chosen One</u>."* (Luke 23:35)

And coming to Him as to a living stone, rejected by men, but <u>choice</u> and precious in the sight of God, (1Peter 2:4)

For this is contained in Scripture: "Behold I lay in Zion a <u>choice</u> stone, a precious corner stone, And he who believes in Him shall not be disappointed." (1Peter 2:6)

Consequently, New Testament believers are chosen through being placed in the *"chosen one"* (Luke 9:35; Isaiah 42:1), Jesus Christ, subsequent to repenting and believing while depraved.

Jesus' Chosenness

The Father's choice of Jesus had nothing to do with Jesus' eternal destiny. In other words, He was not chosen to spend eternity in heaven. His chosenness related to His function in the Father's overall plan—that of serving as Savior.

No Other Candidates

We must be careful not to equate Christ's chosenness with selection. Christ was not selected from a group of candidates qualified to function as Savior. No one but the eternal Son was capable of paying the sin debt. Thus, His chosenness had nothing to do with selection.

Timing of Church Saints' Chosenness

Ephesians 1:4a states that New Testament believers are chosen *"in Him before the foundation of the world."* Does this mean that God selected us for salvation before we were born—selected us to be placed into Christ? Absolutely not!

When we made the choice to accept Christ as Savior (while depraved), we were placed into Christ through the avenue of the Holy Spirit (1Corinthians 12:13), into the Father's *"chosen one"* (Luke 9:35; Isaiah 42:1), and made *"new"* (2Corinthians 5:17). This action by God on our behalf, subsequent to our exercising personal repentance and faith while depraved, allowed us to enter into Christ's chosenness. Once in Christ, we also received His kind of life (Colossians 3:4), eternal life having no beginning and no end. Thus, once we were placed into Christ and received eternal life, the Father saw us as having always been in Christ, even though our point of entry into Christ was <u>after</u> we repented and believed while depraved. This sequence makes it possible for us to have been *"in Him before the foundation of the world,"* even though we did not accept Him until almost two thousand years after the cross. It also leaves room for God's foreknowledge to precede our being chosen (elected) as required by 1 Peter 1:1-2, since we were not placed in Christ (the Father's *"chosen one"* — Isaiah 42:1) until we repented and exercised faith while depraved.

> *...who are chosen* [elected] <u>*according to*</u> *the foreknowledge of God the Father...* (1 Peter 1:1-2)

Are you seeing the necessity of living from the view above — from where you are "in Christ"? Without this view our vision is extremely limited. (We will study Ephesians 1:4 in greater depth later in this series. So, for now, glean what you can and trust God with the remainder.)

Little Messiahs or Holy and Blameless Saints

Christ was chosen to be Messiah. This means that once we were placed in Him and made new (after repenting and believing while depraved), we entered into His chosenness. But, we, by no means, have become little Messiahs. We have become *"holy and blameless"* saints, as the following phrase from Ephesians 1:4 confirms:

> *...that we should be holy and blameless before Him...* (Ephesians 1:4)

Living by Christ's Life

Jesus was also chosen to display the Father's character to the world (John 14:9-10). In fact, He (God-man) lived by the Father's very life, meaning that He came to do more than die on a cross as Savior. He came to demonstrate what man would look like should man choose to live by His life. Actually, He died so He could continue doing, during the church age, what He had done during His First Coming — which is live, on earth, by the Father's life. He lives in this manner today when New Testament believers yield to His life through the peaks and valleys of daily living (Romans 6:13). In such cases, the Father, living through the Son, accomplishes the work done through all church saints from Acts 2 through the Rapture. What an amazing plan, a plan that Paul understood well according to Romans 5:10!

> *For if while we were enemies, we were reconciled to God through*
> *the death of His Son, much more, having been reconciled, we shall*
> *be <u>saved by His life</u>.* (Romans 5:10)

Jesus died not only to provide a way of escape for unredeemed mankind, but to also create a situation where He, living inside every believer during the church age (Galatians 2:20; Colossians 3:4), could continue to demonstrate the Father's character through those in pursuit of His heart. This truth explains why Paul's goal was intimacy with the Creator (Philippians 3:10) rather than activity. Such intimacy, however, results in one of the most active lifestyles imaginable because God alone, never man, empowers it. Note Paul's words from 1Corinthians 15:10:

> *But by the grace of God I am what I am, and His grace toward me*
> *did not prove vain; but I labored even more than all of them, yet*
> *not I, but the grace of God with me.* (1Corinthians 15:10)

Truly, our God is an awesome God! Is not the life of faith, lived by the life of Another (God's very life), the most exciting endeavor imaginable?

"Predestined" in Ephesians 1:5, the Contextual View

> *In love (1:4c) He <u>predestined</u> us to adoption as sons through Jesus*
> *Christ to Himself, according to the kind intention of His will*
> (Ephesians 1:5)

All Things Done in Love

Much debate exists as to where the words *"In love"* (Ephesians 1:4c) should be attached. Some think they belong at the end of the previous phrase, *"that we should be holy and blameless before Him"* (Ephesians 1:4). Others view them as relating to the first phrase of verse 5, *"He predestined us to adoption as sons through Jesus Christ to Himself."* The debate exists because verses 3-14 are one sentence in the Greek. The New American Standard Bible attaches *"In love"* (Ephesians 1:4c) to the beginning of Ephesians 1:5, so we will study the passage from that vantage point. Actually, where *"In love"* is attached makes little difference because everything that God does, since His very nature is *"love"* (1John 4:8, 16), is done in unconditional, agape *"love."* Note that the verse does not say "In sovereignty He predestined us to adoption as sons." Yes, God is sovereign, but His love is what motivates Him to give us such a wonderful destiny.

94

Predestination Defined

The word *"predestined"* is interesting indeed. Did God predetermine, through a selection process, and from eternity past, who will go to heaven and who will go to hell? Or is man allowed to choose his eternal destiny for himself? An examination of Ephesians 1:5, phrase-by-phrase, will determine Paul's intent.

When God predestines an individual, He does so *"in love"* (1:4c). What then does Paul mean by the phrase, *"He predestined us"* (Ephesians 1:5)? Is he saying that God predetermined, from eternity past, that a portion of mankind would be saved and the remainder condemned? Such a mindset contradicts 1Timothy 2:4 and 2Peter 3:9, which state that He desires that none *"perish"*—that *"all...come to repentance"* and experience salvation. Is Paul, in Ephesians 1:5, suggesting to his readers that man is incapable of choosing where he will spend eternity? If so, the cross would have been a waste of time for the Father, Son, and the entire Godhead—for the cross represents a choice. For God to select some of mankind to receive salvation, reject those who remain, and follow by sending His Son to Calvary is highly contradictory. In fact, if God is capable of saving all (as even the Calvinists believe), yet only saves some (by predestining and electing each to salvation from eternity past by means of an eternal decree—Calvinism's view), and at the same time desires that all be saved (1Timothy 2:4; 2Peter 3:9), how can He be the emotionally stable, just, loving, and compassionate God described so vividly in the Scriptures? He cannot be that God! Consequently, an alternate way to view the term *"predestined"* must exist. The answer is found in the full counsel of God's Word.

The cross represents man's prerogative to make a choice. In fact, two trees in the history of man confirm that man has been granted the right of choice. One tree was *"the tree of the knowledge of good and evil"* (Genesis 2:17). The other tree was the cross, or *"tree"* of Christ (Galatians 3:13). Predestination, therefore, must indicate something other than God predetermining, or selecting, who will be saved or lost.

Predestined Not to Salvation

As has already been discussed, the word *"predestined"* is used only six times in Scripture (Acts 4:28; Romans 8:29; Romans 8:30; 1Corinthians 2:7; Ephesians 1:5; Ephesians 1:11). Four of these verses are used in reference to the church (Romans 8:29; Romans 8:30; Ephesians 1:5; Ephesians 1:11). When these passages are examined in context, we discover that God did not predestine (from eternity past by means of an eternal decree) certain individuals to become believers. Rather, God mandated that New Testament believers receive a glorious future destiny in association with being placed in Christ after repenting and believing while depraved. Thus, predestination has nothing to do with who will become believers, for it has everything to do with a person's future destiny once he/she exercises repentance and faith (while depraved) and is placed in Christ. Consequently, New Testament believers are predestined when the Holy Spirit places them in Christ, after they choose to repent and believe while depraved.

Consider the following, noticing again that I repeat myself quite often by saying the same thing in a variety of ways. I have found this to be a profitable tool when communicating truths that are somewhat controversial.

Predestined to *"Adoption as Sons"*

The phrase, *"predestined us to adoption as sons"* (Ephesians 1:5a), along with Romans 8:23, help validate that a person is not predestined until he/she is placed in Christ subsequent to exercising personal repentance and faith while depraved. We will confirm this truth by first reading Ephesians 1:5:

> *He predestined us to adoption as sons through Jesus Christ to*
> *Himself, according to the kind intention of His will* (Ephesians 1:5)

The word crucial to a correct understanding is the first word after *"predestined"* in Ephesians 1:5a, the word *"us."* Since Paul, a fellow believer, wrote the epistle of Ephesians to church saints, the term *"us"* refers to New Testament believers. Consequently, New Testament believers (once they are made new after repenting and believing while depraved) are the ones predestined—*"He predestined us...."* To what are they predestined? They are *"predestined...to adoption as sons"* (Ephesians 1:5a). To what does this phrase make reference? Romans 8:23 provides the answer:

> *And not only this, but also we ourselves, having the first fruits of*
> *the Spirit, even we ourselves groan within ourselves, waiting*
> *eagerly for <u>our adoption as sons</u>, <u>the redemption of our body</u>*
> *(underline for emphasis).* (Romans 8:23)

The *"adoption as sons"* (Romans 8:23) will occur when all members of the church age receive their new bodies, which will also fulfill the phrase, *"the redemption of our body"* (Romans 8:23). This wonderful event will transpire long after most New Testament believers are saved/justified (except in the case of those who are saved/justified shortly before the Rapture of the church). Therefore, New Testament believers are *"predestined"* when they are placed in Christ and made new creations subsequent to repenting and believing while depraved. They, consequently, were not *"predestined"* to be saved/justified, but rather are *"predestined... to adoption as sons"* (Ephesians 1:5) in conjunction with being saved/justified. This sequence means that even Paul has not yet experienced the *"adoption as sons."* Paul's adoption as a son will not take place until his body, along with the bodies of all church saints, is resurrected in accordance with 1Thessalonians 4:13-18 and 1Corinthians 15:35-58—verses that address the Rapture of the church.

"Adoption as Sons": The Resurrection of Church Saints' Bodies

The members of the body of Christ are not adopted as sons in the fullest sense until their bodies are resurrected:

> *"And not only this, but also we ourselves, having <u>the first fruits of the Spirit</u>, even we ourselves groan within ourselves, waiting eagerly for <u>our adoption as sons, the redemption of our body</u>."*
> (Romans 8:23)

Church saints now have *"the first fruits of the Spirit"* (Romans 8:23), *"a spirit of adoption as sons"* (Romans 8:15):

> *"For you have not received a spirit of slavery leading to fear again, but you have received <u>a spirit of adoption as sons</u> by which we cry out, 'Abba! Father!'"* (Romans 8:15)

New Testament believers, having received *"a spirit of adoption as sons"* (Romans 8:15), are *"sons"* (Romans 8:14; Galatians 4:5-7) who are *"led by the Spirit of God"* (Romans 8:14). As a result of possessing the Holy Spirit, they have already received the down payment (*"first fruits,"* or earnest—the divine engagement ring) of what is to come (Romans 8:23). However, only when their bodies are resurrected (1Thessalonians 4:13-18) will they lay hold, in the fullest sense, of all that this sonship involves.

Conclusions to be Drawn

Believers today, not yet having received resurrected bodies, have received *"a spirit of adoption as sons"* (Romans 8:15). We are holy, blameless, complete, justified, redeemed, forgiven, children of God who are being taught and trained by God's Spirit. One day we will receive our new bodies, at which time we will obtain that for which we have patiently waited, the *"adoption as sons"* (Ephesians 1:5; Romans 8:23). We will have been *"holy and blameless"* in our persons (in our souls and spirits) since the day we believed and were ushered into God's family (Ephesians 1:4). After our bodies are resurrected, however, we will be holy and blameless in soul, spirit, and body.

This transformation means that, for the first time in our existence, every aspect of our being will be totally perfected. Why? The power of sin, which lived in our earthly bodies (Romans 7:23), will not reside in our resurrected bodies. Also, our brains, which stored unrighteous habit patterns (and godly habit patterns as well), will be replaced with brains free of the unrighteous patterns. As a result of the Spirit's training while in our earthly bodies, along with the training received in heaven prior to Christ's Second Coming, we will be mature saints when we return with the Lord (in our resurrected bodies) to reign with Him during the Millennium (Revelation 20:4). Even after we have received our new bodies at the Rapture of the church (the Rapture occurring prior to the Tribulation and Christ's Second Coming), and later begin to *"reign"* (Revelation 20:4), we will be no more holy and blameless in our souls and spirits, and no more a part of God's family, than when we were saved/justified. The following explains why this must be the case.

The Meaning of *"Adoption as Sons"* for the New Testament Believer

If we have chosen to accept Jesus as Savior, we were made full-fledged *"children of God"* (John 1:12) the moment we were spiritually regenerated (justified/saved). The Spirit brings us to maturity, preparing us for the day when we will reign with Christ. However, we will not reign while we are in our earthly bodies. But when the *"mortal"* puts on *"immortality"* (1Corinthians 15:51-53), we will not only be fully adopted *"as sons"* (Ephesians 1:5; Romans 8:23), but be better equipped to reign with the Master.

Paul states:

> *"And because you are sons, God has sent forth the Spirit of His Son into our hearts, crying, 'Abba! Father!'"* (Galatians 4:6)

Did you hear that? The Holy Spirit enters *"our hearts, crying, 'Abba! Father!'"* In other words, He makes us mindful of the fact that Jehovah God is our Father. The Holy Spirit, in crying, *"Abba! Father!,"* also brings awareness that salvation includes much more than God getting us out of hell and into heaven. It allows the New Testament believer to see that one day he/she will be, in the fullest sense, adopted as a son—receive the *"adoption as sons"* that Paul addresses in Ephesians 1:5 and Romans 8:23. Paul tells the Galatians:

> *in order that He might redeem those who were under the Law, that*
> *we might receive the <u>adoption as sons</u>.* (Galatians 4:5)

Yes, God not only redeemed us (Galatians 4:5) and gave us *"a spirit of adoption as sons"* (Romans 8:15), but He also granted us the privilege of one day being fully adopted *"as sons"* (Galatians 4:5) through the resurrection of our bodies (Romans 8:23):

> *And not only this, but also we ourselves, having the first fruits of*
> *the Spirit, even we ourselves groan within ourselves, waiting*
> *eagerly for our <u>adoption as sons</u>, <u>the redemption of our body</u>.*
> (Romans 8:23)

The phrase, *"that we might receive"* (Galatians 4:5), is in the subjunctive mood—a mood in the Greek language that cannot indicate time of action. We must go elsewhere to determine <u>when</u> this action takes place in regard to the New Testament believer's *"adoption as sons"* (Galatians 4:5). Romans 8:23 tells us that it occurs when we receive our glorified bodies at the Rapture of the church. No doubt, our *"adoption as sons"* is a <u>future</u> occurrence, which refutes the argument that it points to that time when a person is saved (justified). Also, in 2Corinthians 3:18, we find that one of the Spirit's main purposes is to bring church saints to maturity so they can better experience all that sonship provides.

What We Have Learned Regarding *"Adoption as Sons"*

When Paul stated, *"He predestined us to adoption as sons"* (Ephesians 1:5a), he realized that becoming an adopted son in the fullest sense would transpire in the <u>future</u>. It remains a future event for us as well. Consequently, to be predestined *"to adoption as sons"* does <u>not</u> mean that we were predestined from eternity past, by means of an eternal decree, to be saved. Rather, it communicates that in conjunction with being saved (subsequent to repenting and believing while depraved), we were granted a glorious future destiny—that of one day being adopted as a son in fullest measure (Ephesians 1:5a). At that time (when the Rapture occurs), church saints will be conformed to the image of Christ in every respect (in soul, spirit, <u>and body</u>—Romans 8:29). What great news!

Jesus was and is *"the first-born from the dead"* (Colossians 1:18; Revelation 1:5) and *"the first-born among many brethren"* (Romans 8:29). Even though Jesus has always been the eternal Son of God, He was *"declared the Son of God with power"* (Romans 1:4) through His resurrection. Fittingly, we will receive the *"adoption as sons"* (Ephesians 1:5a) through the avenue of the resurrection of our bodies. We were predestined to this transformation (granted this glorious future destiny) when (not before) we were placed in Christ after repenting and believing while depraved.

Predestined to Adoption *"According to the Kind Intention of His Will"*

God granted us this glorious future destiny *"according to the kind intention of His will"* (Ephesians 1:5b). God is not, therefore, an angry tyrant who gains pleasure from harassing His people and condemning the unjust to hell. God's intentions are *"kind"* toward those who are His. He even loves the lost who reject His gracious offer of salvation (John 3:16), saving them should they choose (while depraved) to repent and believe. Once we grasp this truth, we can better comprehend why *"faith...works"* most efficiently through *"love"* (Galatians 5:6). We can also understand why *"the love of Christ"* — not law, a sense of duty, or fear of God's wrath — is the greatest motivator of all (2Corinthians 5:14):

> *For in Christ Jesus neither circumcision nor uncircumcision means*
> *anything, but faith working through love.* (Galatians 5:6)

> *For the love of Christ controls us...*(2Corinthians 5:14)

If you have viewed God differently than He is described here, won't you allow His Word to reshape your thinking?

> *to the praise of the glory of His grace, which He freely bestowed*
> *on us in the Beloved.* (Ephesians 1:6)

God *"predestined us to adoption as sons through Jesus Christ to Himself"* (Ephesians 1:5a) *"to the praise of the glory of His grace"* (Ephesians 1:6a). The fact that God would give the New Testament believer such a delightful future destiny should result in *"praise"* from all church saints. The word *"which"* (Ephesians 1:6b) refers to *"grace"* (Ephesians 1:6a), the *"grace"* that allowed God to predestine us *"to adoption as sons"* (Ephesians 1:5a) when He placed us in Christ subsequent to our repenting and believing while depraved. The word *"Beloved"* (Ephesians 1:6b) makes reference to Jesus, *"in"* Whom New Testament believers receive this *"grace."* Combining these factors, and considering that we were saved/justified through being placed *"in the Beloved"* (2Corinthians 5:17 1Corinthians 12:13; Ephesians 1:6b) after choosing to repent and believe, compels us to correctly conclude that we were not predestined until we were placed *"in the Beloved"* (after repenting and believing while depraved).

For the sake of time and space, we will skip down to Ephesians 1:11 and examine how Paul uses the term *"predestined"* for the last time in the New Testament.   Do you think it will line up with what we have previously discovered? If God's Word is absolute truth, void of contradiction, it should fit like a glove.

"Predestined" in Ephesians 1:11, the Contextual View

In Him (Ephesians 1:10) *also we have obtained an inheritance,*
having been <u>*predestined*</u> *according to His purpose who works all*
things after the counsel of His will (Ephesians 1:11)

Note that the two words, *"In Him,"* included in the last phrase of Ephesians 1:10, tie in with the first statement of verse 11.

The Value of Being God's Inheritance

The statement, *"In Him* (1:10) *also we have obtained an inheritance"* (1:11), is particularly encouraging; for the phrase, *"we have obtained an inheritance,"* can be interpreted, *"we have been made a heritage,"* or, *"we were made an inheritance."* Regardless of which rendering we choose, the passage does not contradict teachings elsewhere in the Scriptures.   No doubt, in Christ we have an inheritance Acts 20:32; Ephesians 1:13-14; Ephesians 5:5; Colossians 1:12; Colossians 3:23-24; Hebrews 9:15; 1Peter 1:3-4).   In fact, we are *"fellow heirs with Christ"* (Romans 8:17), which means that what He owns we own as well.   He is also our inheritance in the sense of being our very life (Colossians 3:4), a rich inheritance indeed.   Neither is there any doubt that in Christ we were made the Father's *"inheritance"* (Ephesians 1:18):

I pray that the eyes of your heart may be enlightened, so that you
may know what is the hope of His calling, what are the riches of
the glory of <u>*His inheritance in the saints*</u>, (Ephesians 1:18)

To have been placed *"in Christ"* (1Corinthians 1:30), Who is the Father's Son, and not be the Father's inheritance, is impossible!

Numerous scholars view the proper rendering of the phrase, *"we have obtained an inheritance"* (Ephesians 1:11), as, *"we were made an inheritance."*   Just think what this means! We are valued so highly that the Father views us as His very own inheritance.   I don't know about you, but when I think *"inheritance"* I think "special."   In fact, an inheritance is something to be cherished.   Consequently, the inheritance received from a parent, regardless of how large or small, is precious, priceless, and greatly valued.   The Father views us in this same manner.   To Him we are very special beings, possessing great value, because we are sons. Why then should we consider ourselves as valueless, good-for-nothing, worthless, sinners saved by grace who are nothing more than second-class citizens of the Kingdom? If we think of ourselves in this manner, we have bought a lie. God, through Paul, states that we are His *"inheritance"* (Ephesians 1:11) and are *"holy and blameless before Him"* (Ephesians 1:4). May we bask in the joy and freedom of this truth and never look back!

The Significance of *"Predestined According to His Purpose"*

We discovered in Ephesians 1:5-6 that once God placed us "*in the Beloved*" (after we exercised repentance and faith while depraved), we were *"predestined...to adoption as sons."* Yes, at that time, we were freely granted the wonderful future destiny of one day receiving our new, resurrected bodies (Romans 8:23). When we receive our new, resurrected bodies at the Rapture of the church we will, for the first time, be totally conformed to the image of God's Son (Romans 8:29) in soul, spirit, as well as <u>body</u>. Thus, a New Testament believer is granted this glorious future destiny, with all of its positive ramifications, when he/she exercises repentance and faith, while depraved, and is placed in Christ—not by means of a selection process that occurred from eternity past. Why is this the case? Notice the phrase:

> *having been <u>predestined according to His purpose</u>* (Ephesians 1:11b)

God's purposes are *"eternal"* (Ephesians 3:11):

> *This was in accordance with the* <u>eternal purpose</u> *which He carried out in Christ Jesus our Lord,* (Ephesians 3:11)

(For more input regarding God's eternal purposes, reference **The Key** in th **Introduction**.)

Because God's purposes are eternal, they have always existed within His heart. Thus, if we are *"predestined according to His purpose"* (Ephesians 1:11b), His *"purpose"* must precede our predestination. Why must His *"purpose"* precede ou predestination? The action or entity that follows the words *"according to"* (such a God's *"purpose"* in Ephesians 1:11b) must occur or exist <u>before</u> the action or entit that precedes the words *"according to"* (such as *"predestined"* in Ephesians 1:11 b To state it differently:

102

If **A** is "*according to*" **B**

Then **B** precedes **A**

Thus, God's "*purpose*" (**B**) must precede our predestination (**A**). This means that our predestination occurs in time, subsequent not only to "*His purpose*" (which is "*eternal*" — Ephesians 3:11), but also subsequent to His foreknowledge of our choosing Him (refer to Diagrams 2, 7, and 8 in the Reference Section). This sequence lines up perfectly with Romans 8:29, which requires God's foreknowledge to precede our predestination:

For whom He foreknew, He also predestined... (Romans 8:29)

Note: The words "*according to*" (Ephesians 1:11b) will be discussed in greater depth shortly. Their significance is nothing short of amazing!

Isn't it pleasing to know that our eternal God has always desired that New Testament believers be predestined "*to adoption as sons*" (Ephesians 1:5) in conjunction with the Holy Spirit placing them in Christ (1Corinthians 12:13) subsequent to their choosing to repent and believe while depraved?

God's Will

All that we discovered in Ephesians 1:5 regarding predestination is reaffirmed in Ephesians 1:11-12. In verse 11b Paul states that the New Testament believer has "*been predestined according to His purpose*," and in verse 12 he states that purpose. We will tie Ephesians 1:11b in with Ephesians 1:12 shortly, but before doing so we must deal with the phrase:

> *who works all things after the counsel of His will* (Ephesians 1:11c)

Ephesians 1:11c does <u>not</u> teach that all events are determined by God's will. The word "*works*," from the Greek word *energeo* ("to be at work, to work, to do"), can also be interpreted "energizes." Thus, God "*energizes all things after the <u>counsel</u> of his will*." The word "*counsel*" plays a major role in determining what Paul is communicating here, as confirmed by Dave Hunt in *What Love Is This?*, page 172:

> In light of such scriptures, how can we understand the statement
> that God works "all things according to the counsel of His own
> will" (Ephesians 1:11)? Alvin Baker claims that this passage
> proves that "God works 'all things,' including sin, according to His

103

eternal will." However, the word "worketh" (KJV) is *energeo*, which doesn't convey the idea of controlled manipulation but of stimulation. See Colossians 1:29 and 2 Thessalonians 2:7,9; see also "work out your own salvation...for it is God which worketh in [energizes] you" (Philippians 2:12–13).

Nor does Paul say that God works all according to His will, but according to the *counsel* of His will. There is a huge difference. Obviously, the eternal "counsel" of His will must have allowed man the freedom to love and obey, or to defy, his Creator— otherwise sin would be God's will. We could never conclude from this passage (and particularly not in light of the many scriptures stating that men defy God's will) that mankind's every thought, word, and deed is according to God's perfect will, exactly the way God desired and decreed it. Yet that is what Calvinists erroneously conclude from Ephesians 1:11. To make that the case, as Calvin did, portrays God as the effective cause of every sin ever committed.

Christ asks us to pray, "Thy kingdom come Thy will be done in earth, as it is in heaven" (Matthew 6:10; Luke 11:2). Why would Christ suggest such a prayer, if everything is already according to God's will and His eternal decree—and if we are already in the kingdom of God with Satan bound, as both Calvin and Augustine taught?

The objection is raised: "How dare you suggest that the omnipotent God cannot effect His will!" Of course He can and does, but that in itself does not say that God wills everything that happens. Without freedom to do his own will, man would not be a morally responsible being, nor could he be guilty of sin. That much is axiomatic.

Christ's special commendation of "whosoever shall do the will of my Father" (Matthew 12:50; Mark 3:35), and such statements from His lips as "Not every one that saith unto me, Lord, Lord, shall enter into the kingdom of heaven; but he that doeth the will of my Father" (Matthew 7:21), show very clearly that everyone doesn't always fulfill God's will. The same truth is found in Isaiah 65:12, 1 Thessalonians 5:17–22, Hebrews 10:36, 1 Peter 2:15–16, 1 John 2:17 and elsewhere. Clearly, there is a distinction between what God desires and wills, and what He *allows*.[38]

Hunt's assessment of Ephesians 1:11c is quite interesting. In fact, I agree with his conclusions. Let's consider some of the verses he references, beginning with Colossians 1:29:

> *And for this purpose also I labor, striving according to His power,*
> *which mightily <u>works</u> within me.* (Colossians 1:29)

The word *"works"* is *energeia*, which is from the same Greek root word as *"works"* in Ephesians 1:11. This fact allows Colossians 1:29 to be rendered as follows:

> *"And for this purpose also I labor, striving according to His power,*
> *which mightily <u>energizes</u> within me."* (Colossians 1:29)

This positive energizing is done by God, and is a stimulation—not a "controlled manipulation" (to use Hunts words). Even in Philippians 2:13, 1Corinthians 12:6 (and an assortment of additional passages), Paul teaches that God works in, or energizes, those who are His. Does <u>all</u> energizing come from God? Not according to 2Thessalonians 2:9:

> *"that is, the one whose coming is in accord with the <u>activity</u> of*
> *Satan, with all power and signs and false wonders."*
> (2Thessalonians 2:9)

The word *"activity"* in 2Thessalonians 2:9 can be viewed as an energizing since it is from the Greek word *energeia* (the same as in Colossians 1:29), meaning "operative power." Thus, Satan also energizes whomever he can in an attempt to thwart God's ultimate plan (the plan described in Ephesians 1:10—that of *"summing up...all things in Christ"*). Also consider Ephesians 2:1-2, realizing that the word *"working"* is from the Greek word *energeo*, as in Ephesians 1:11:

> *And you were dead in your trespasses and sins, in which you*
> *formerly walked according to the course of this world, according to*
> *the prince of the power of the air, of the spirit that is now <u>working</u> in*
> *the sons of disobedience.* (Ephesians 2:1-2)

Since both God and Satan are in the business of energizing, the believer must make sure to yield to the proper energy source. Consequently, Ephesians 1:11c cannot be communicating that God works (energizes) all things, since 2Thessalonians 2:9 and Ephesians 2:1-2 confirm that Satan energizes as well.

The words *"all things"* in the phrase *"who works all things after the counsel of His will"* (Ephesians 1:11c) cannot mean *"all events"* or *"all that transpires"* because Luke states:

> *"For the Pharisees and the lawyers rejected God's purpose for*
> *themselves, not having been baptized by John."* (Luke 7:30)

We learn here that God's ultimate strategy for the universe will prevail even though some individuals reject His *"purpose for themselves."* No doubt, God desires that none perish:

> *who desires all men to be saved and to come to the knowledge of the truth.* (1Timothy 2:4)

> *"The Lord is not slow about His promise, as some count slowness, but is patient toward you, not wishing for any to perish but for all to come to repentance"* (2Peter 3:9).

Thus, if a man perishes, it is due to his own choice. The Father would relish the idea of having all mankind accept His Son and enter into *"the summing up of all things in Christ"* (Ephesians 1:10)—an event which occurs in the distant future. We know, however, that man's rebellion against his Creator will prevent universal salvation from occurring.

Rejection of God's Will

God requires a choice on man's part, while man is depraved, before granting salvation. But, the *"will"* of God, which is addressed in Ephesians 1:11c, *"who works all things after the counsel of His will,"* can be rejected by man. In other words, God may will something for an individual that the individual rejects. Jesus confirms this truth in Matthew 23:37:

> *"How often I wanted to gather your children together, the way a hen gathers her chicks under her wings, and you were <u>unwilling</u>"* (Matthew 23:37).

(Note: Matthew 23:37 is covered in depth in *God's Heart as it Relates to Depravity*, the third book of this *God's Heart* series, but is only referenced here.)

Man has a free will and can choose what he desires, as also verified by the last sentence in Isaiah 65:12:

> *And you did evil in My sight, <u>and chose that in which I did not delight.</u>"* (Isaiah 65:12)

Regardless of how many (or how few) choose to obey, God's ultimate will and strategy of *"summing up...all things in Christ"* (Ephesians 1:10) cannot be thwarted. Thus, the phrase, *"who works all things after the counsel of His will*

(Ephesians 1:11c), is not communicating that God wills all things—that man is incapable of making choices outside of God's will. Let's follow Paul's train of thought by addressing Ephesians 1:12.

> *to the end that we who were the first to hope in Christ should be to*
> *the praise of His glory.* (Ephesians 1:12)

The Phillips translation interprets the last phrase of this verse as, "*may bring praise to His glory.*" This last phrase confirms that New Testament believers, who have become God's *"inheritance"* (Ephesians 1:11a), and are *"predestined"* (Ephesians 1:11b) *"to adoption as sons"* (Ephesians 1:5a), will *"bring praise to "His glory"* (Ephesians 1:12 Phillips). What else could result if, after receiving our resurrected bodies (that to which we were predestined once we were placed in Christ subsequent to repenting and believing while depraved—Ephesians 1:5-6; Romans 8:23), we return with Christ as His body and bride? Yes, much glory will be directed toward the Father when Christ returns. As we discussed earlier, if Jesus glorified the Father at His First Coming, just imagine how much the Father will be glorified when Jesus returns with His glorified body, made up of church saints *"conformed to"* His *"image"* (Romans 8:29). Thus, the Son's return will bring glory to the Father, once again confirming that the Son does everything for the benefit of others—in this case His Father.

Reformed Theology, due to viewing the depraved as incapable of exercising repentance and faith, perceive predestination to salvation from eternity past a necessity. However, Philippians 2:10-11 teaches that a time will come when the unsaved/depraved will bow and confess Jesus as Lord:

> *that at the name of Jesus every knee should bow, of those who are*
> *in heaven, and on earth, and under the earth, and that every tongue*
> *should confess that Jesus Christ is Lord, to the glory of God the*
> *Father.* (Philippians 2:10-11)

Thus, Philippians 2:10-11 disproves the contradictory teaching that portrays the depraved (the spiritually unregenerated) as incapable of confessing *"that Jesus Christ is Lord."* In fact, this erroneous mindset views the depraved as spiritual corpses, incapable of responding to any type of spiritual stimulus. However, the lost (depraved) present in Philippians 2:8-11 (all the lost, of all the ages) will not be spiritually regenerated, yet will confess Jesus as Lord. This confession will not result in salvation, for they will receive God's wrath for failing to repent and believe while depraved during their stay on the earth (Revelation 20:11-15).

Before leaving our study of **The Contextual View Of *"Predestined,"*** we need to look more closely at two words that have been linked together in the Scriptures for a very special purpose. The two words are *"according to."* They shed tremendous light on the subject of predestination and, in fact, are among the major players in determining <u>when</u> predestination occurs. Prepare yourself to be blessed. Understanding the significance of these two words is much ammunition for those who view God as predestining New Testament believers to blessings associated with salvation, once He places them in Christ subsequent to their repenting and believing while depraved, rather than predestining certain persons to salvation from eternity past by means of an eternal decree.

C H A P T E R   E I G H T

II. THE AWESOMENESS OF *"ACCORDING TO"*

THE WORDS, *"ACCORDING TO,"* are employed 790 times in the New American Standard Bible, 725 in the King James, and on occasion are found more than once in some verses. They are used in relation to predestination in Ephesians 1:11, a verse addressed earlier:

> ... *having been predestined <u>according to</u> His purpose who works all things after the counsel of His will,* (Ephesians 1:11)

No doubt, the believer is *"predestined according to His purpose,"* God's *"purpose"*—which means that God's *"purpose,"* which is *"eternal"* (Ephesians 3:11), must <u>precede</u> the believer's predestination. Why is this the case? The action or entity that follows the words *"according to"* (such as God's *"purpose"* in Ephesians 1:11) must occur (or exist) <u>before</u> the action or entity that precedes the words *"according to"* (such as *"predestined"* in Ephesians 1:11). Consequently:

If A is <u>according to</u> B

Then B <u>precedes</u> A

This principle applies in every instance where *"according to"* is used in the Scriptures. Should you look up each reference, you would be amazed at the consistency of God's Word. Some examples are listed below. (Note: For the purpose of emphasis, the words *"according to"* are underlined in each of the following passages.)

109

> *Then God said, "Let Us make man in Our image, <u>according to</u> Our likeness;* (Genesis 1:26)

Because the Triune God existed before *"man"* was made (created), *"Our"* (pointing to God) <u>follows</u> the phrase *"according to,"* while *"man"* <u>precedes</u> it.

> *Thus Noah did; <u>according to</u> all that God had commanded him, so he did.* (Genesis 6:22)

What *"God...commanded"* preceded Noah's obedience.

> *To each one he interpreted <u>according to</u> his own dream.* (Genesis 41:12)

The *"dream"* existed before the interpretation.

> *And the LORD did <u>according to</u> the word of Moses,* (Exodus 8:13)

Moses' words were spoken before the Lord responded *("did")*.

> *Then you shall erect the tabernacle <u>according to</u> its plan...*(Exodus 26:30)

The *"plan"* for the tabernacle existed before *"the tabernacle"* was erected.

> *So they did <u>according to</u> the word of Moses.* (Leviticus 10:7)

Moses spoke *"the word"* before the people *"did"* what he had spoken.

> *Thus the sons of Israel did; <u>according to</u> all that the LORD commanded Moses...*(Numbers 2:34)

"All that the Lord commanded Moses" existed before *"the sons of Israel did"* what He had commanded.

> *"Be careful against an infection of leprosy, that you diligently observe and do <u>according to</u> all that the Levitical priests shall teach you;...* (Deuteronomy 24:8)

The teaching preceded the observance of the teaching.

> *This book of the law shall not depart from your mouth, but you shall meditate on it day and night, so that you may be careful to do <u>according to</u> all that is written in it;...* (Joshua 1:8)

"The law" had to be *"written"* before the people could observe what was written.

> *...May the LORD repay the evildoer <u>according to</u> his evil."* (2Samuel 3:39)

The *"evil"* was committed before *"the evildoer"* was repaid.

> *To this day they do <u>according to</u> the earlier customs:...* (2Kings 17:34)

The *"customs"* existed before the nation observed them.

> *Then Ezra rose and made the leading priests, the Levites, and all Israel, take oath that they would do <u>according to</u> this proposal; so they took the oath.*
> (Ezra 10:5)

The *"proposal"* existed before the *"oath"* could be taken.

> *...Then the people did <u>according to</u> this promise.* (Nehemiah 5:13)

The *"promise"* existed before *"the people did"* what the promise required.

> *...and it was written <u>according to</u> all that Mordecai commanded to the Jews,...* (Esther 8:9)

That which *"Mordecai commanded"* existed before what *"was written."*

> *"For He pays a man <u>according to</u> his work,...* (Job 34:11)

"Work" is done before payment can be received.

> *...Deliver me <u>according to</u> Thy word.* (Psalm 119:170)

God's *"word"* existed before deliverance was requested.

> *...And I will make an everlasting covenant with you, <u>According to</u> the faithful mercies shown to David.* (Isaiah 55:3)

The *"mercies shown to David"* existed before the *"covenant"* was made.

> *...Repay her <u>according to</u> her work;...* (Jeremiah 50:29)

The *"work"* preceded the repayment.

> *...but have acted <u>according to</u> the ordinances of the nations around you.* (Ezekiel 11:12)

"The ordinances of the nations" existed before actions were taken.

> *...But He does according to His will...* (Daniel 4:35)

God's *"will"* exists before He acts.

> *...and will then recompense every man <u>according to</u> his deeds.* (Matthew 16:27)

"Deeds" will be performed before *"recompense"* will be paid

> *...they went up there <u>according to</u> the custom of the Feast;* (Luke 2:42)

> *"The custom of the Feast"* existed before *"they went up."*
> *Pilate therefore said to them, "Take Him yourselves, and judge*
> *Him <u>according to</u> your law."* (John 18:31)

The *"law"* existed before judgment could occur.

> *...nor to walk <u>according to</u> the customs.* (Acts 21:21-22)

"Customs" must exist before a person can *"walk"* in them.

> *...to those who are called <u>according to</u> His purpose.* (Romans
> 8:28)

God's *"purpose,"* which is *"eternal"* (Ephesians 3:11), precedes the New Testament believer's calling. *"Called"* in this case points to the special position or office church saints receive once they are placed in Christ and made new, <u>after</u> having exercised repentance and faith while depraved.

> *for though the twins were not yet born, and had not done anything*
> *good or bad, in order that God's purpose <u>according to</u> His choice*
> *might stand,...* (Romans 9:11)

The wording of this verse differs from the norm. On the surface it seems to communicate that God's *"choice"* precedes His *"purpose,"* but it actually confirms that His *"purpose"* precedes His *"choice."* Because *"might stand"* relates to the word *"purpose,"* Paul is actually saying that God's *"choice"* was made <u>after</u> His *"purpose"* already existed—and that it was made so His *"purpose...might stand."* John Piper (a Reformed theologian) agrees, although he renders *"choice"* as election:

> ....In Rom 9:11c Paul says that God elected Jacob and not Esau "in
> order that the purpose of God according to election might remain."
> (*The Justification of God*, page 49)[39]

Even the English Standard Version renders this phrase as:

> *...in order that God's purpose of election might continue,...*
> (Romans 9:11 ESV)

113

John MacArthur, a Reformed theologian, also agrees. Note his commentary on Romans 9:11 in *The MacArthur Study Bible*:

> Rather, God's choice of Jacob resides solely in His own sovereign plan....[40]

Wayne Grudem, a Reformed theologian as well, writes on page 287 of *Bible doctrine*:

> Nothing that Jacob or Esau would do in life influenced God's decision; it was simply in order that his purpose of election might continue.[41]

Romans 9:11 is in agreement with Ephesians 3:11, which teaches that God's purposes are *"eternal."* No doubt, Romans 9:11 verifies that God's purpose, which is eternal, precedes His *"choice."* (Romans 9:11 is covered in greater depth in *God's Heart as it Relates to Sovereignty/Free Will*, the second book of this *God's Heart* series.)

We will now transition into Romans 11:5, an intriguing verse indeed:

> *In the same way then, there has also come to be at the present time a remnant <u>according to</u> God's gracious choice.* (Romans 11:5 NASB)

Calvinists frequently use this passage in an attempt to verify that God elected (chose) from eternity past, and by means of an eternal decree, individual persons to salvation. One major point must be addressed before drawing our conclusion regarding the verse. In the phrase, *"according to God's gracious choice,"* *"God's"* is italicized in the NASB, signifying its absence in the original Greek text. Also the words, *"gracious choice,"* can be rendered *"choice of grace"* (as indicated in the margin of my NASB and substantiated by the Greek). Therefore, the passage can be written as follows:

> *In the same way then, there has also come to be at the present time a remnant <u>according to</u> the choice of grace.* (Romans 11:5)

This explanation clarifies why the King James Version renders the verse:

> *Even so then at this present time also there is a remnant <u>according to</u> the election of grace.* (Romans 11:5 KJV)

Note: The KJV can insert the word *"election"* in place of *"choice"* (NASB), because *"election"* and *"choice"* are synonyms.

Considering this vital input, we can draw some solid conclusions. Because Romans 11:1-7 addresses truth relating to the Jewish *"people,"* Romans 11:5 has to do with the *"remnant"* of believers within the physical nation of Israel. Don't miss the fact that Paul contrasts faith and grace with works and law, not only in Romans 11 (such as in verse 6), but in other sections of the book of Romans (read Romans 3:27-28, Romans 4:5, and Romans 9:32 for starters). A right standing with God is always based on faith and grace—never works and law. This truth explains why Paul teaches the following in Romans 11:5-7a:

> In the same way then, there has also come to be at the present time
> a remnant <u>according to</u> God's gracious choice. But if it is by
> grace, it is no longer on the basis of works, otherwise grace is no
> longer grace. What then? That which Israel is seeking for, it has
> not obtained, but those who were chosen obtained it,... (Romans
> 11:5-7a NASB)

The right standing with God that the physical nation of Israel pursued could be realized only through what God had prescribed. He had prescribed faith and grace—not works and law. The Jews failed to understand this truth, which causes our study to become enormously interesting. Follow closely.

The physical nation of Israel was chosen (elected) by God to fulfill a specific office—that of a kingdom of priests (Exodus 19:6) who were to take the good news of the Messiah to the Gentiles, the Messiah Who would be born a Jew. The nation's history of rebellion and unrighteousness confirms that God did <u>not</u> choose (elect) her to salvation. But the unbelieving Jewish leaders (rabbis) incorrectly taught that a person entered into the chosenness (election) of the nation of Israel, and received a right standing with God, either by birth or by choice. According to their theology, Jews were part of God's family due to being born into the nation. They also believed that Gentiles could be right with God only through choosing to become a proselyte to Judaism.

Paul strongly refuted this idea by teaching that the chosenness (election) of the nation (Israel) to the office of a kingdom of priests did not result in salvation for a single Jew. The Jews of his day, just as now, needed to enter into the *"election of grace"* (KJV)—which God bestows upon <u>all</u> individuals during the church age who exercise personal repentance and faith while depraved. In fact, all persons who repent and believe during the church age are instantaneously placed in Christ by the Holy Spirit (1Corinthians 12:13) and made new (2Corinthians 5:17). As a result of being placed in the *"chosen one"* of Isaiah 42:1 (NASB), the *"Elect one"* of Isaiah 42:1 (NKJV), they also enter into His chosenness (election). Jesus, of course, was not elected (chosen) to salvation, but was elected (chosen) to the office of

115

Messiah—a very special position (office) indeed. Thus, once New Testament believers are placed into Christ and become part of His body (1Corinthians 12:18-20), they enter into His election (chosenness) and receive a special position (office) as well. This position (office) is used by God to accomplish His purposes, just as Jesus was chosen (elected) as Messiah to accomplish, through the Father's strength, the most important purpose of all. With this in mind, let's again read Romans 11:5:

> *Even so then at this present time also there is a remnant <u>according</u>*
> <u>*to*</u> *the election of grace.* (Romans 11:5 KJV)

Note: Because the following subject matter will be addressed when we study the "U" of the TULIP, Unconditional Election, in *God's Heart as it Relates to Election/Atonement/Grace/ Perseverance* (the fourth book of this *God's Heart* series), digest what you can and leave the remainder for later. Realize, however, that by the time we complete our independent study of election, later in this series, the following input will be very familiar territory and, thus, easily understood.

The *"remnant"* (Romans 11:5) refers to the Jews who, during Paul's day (*"at this present time"*), had made a choice to accept Jesus as Savior. As a result of this choice (exercised in their depravity), the Father, through His *"grace,"* had placed them into Christ, His *"Elect"* [chosen] *One"* (Isaiah 42:1 NKJV), and elected them. Through this means the believing remnant of Jews in Paul's day had entered into the *"the election of grace"* (Romans 11:5 KJV). (Note: Review #2 under **Depravity** in the **Introduction** to understand how depravity applies.)

The Hebrew people were elected (chosen) as *"a kingdom of priests"* (Exodus 19:5-6). Yet, this election did <u>not</u> mean that they were elected (or chosen) to salvation. Rather, it meant that they were elected to fulfill a specific office—that of taking the message of the Messiah to the Gentiles. To enter into the *"election of grace"* (Romans 11:5 KJV) is totally different, for it comes about through God electing those (by His grace) who first exercise repentance and faith while depraved. During the church age, therefore, Jews and Gentiles (who exercise repentance and faith while depraved) are not only placed into the *"Elect* [chosen] *One"* of Isaiah 42:1 (NKJV), Jesus Himself, but also enter into His election (chosenness). Jesus was <u>not</u> elected (chosen) to salvation, but to be Messiah—a very special office indeed. Consequently, New Testament believers, once they exercise personal repentance and faith while depraved and are placed in Christ, enter into Christ's election. The fruit of this election is a special office (position) within His body, the church. This wonderful plan is the means through which New Testament

> *The fruit of election is a special office (position) within His body, the church.*

believers, Jews as well as Gentiles, enter into the *"election of grace"* (KJV) addressed in Romans 11:5.

Thus, *"election"* (Romans 11:5 KJV) does not point to the falsehood that God elected each of the "elect" to <u>salvation</u> from eternity past, by means of an eternal decree. *"Election"* makes reference to the special office that each New Testament believer receives through being placed in the Father's *"Elect* [chosen] *One"* (Isaiah 42:1 NKJV), Jesus the Messiah, subsequent to exercising repentance and faith while depraved. In Paul's day, therefore, Jews were required to choose, while depraved, to accept *"grace"* over Law <u>before</u> God would make them part of the believing *"remnant"* of the nation that entered into *"the election of grace"* addressed in Romans 11:5. The same requirement applies today. Once a Jew accepts Jesus as Savior, God makes him/her not only a member of Christ's body, but also part of the believing *"remnant"* of the Jewish nation.

Let's read Romans 11:5 once more with this remarkable truth in mind:

> *Even so then at this present time also there is a remnant <u>according to</u> the election of grace.* (Romans 11:5 KJV)

Again, we see that if "A" is *"according to"* "B," "B" always <u>precedes</u> "A." In Romans 11:5, "A" is the believing *"remnant"* within the physical nation of Israel in Paul's day (*"at this present time"*), while "B" is *"the election of grace."* Consequently, a Jew in Paul's day had to repent and believe while depraved, and enter into *"the election of grace"* ("B") through being placed in Christ, <u>before</u> becoming part of the *"remnant"* ("A"). The same principle applies throughout the church age. This verse does <u>not</u> teach that God did the choosing from eternity past, by means of an eternal decree, as to who would or would not be saved.

Let's take what we have discussed and apply it to 1Peter 1:1-2:

> *...who are chosen... <u>according to</u> the foreknowledge of God the Father,...* (1Peter 1:1-2 NASB)

> *...Elect... according to the foreknowledge of God the Father...* (1Peter 1:1-2KJV)

This verse confirms that God's *"foreknowledge"* must <u>precede</u> the New Testament believer's election (chosenness), for "B" always precedes "A" when "A" is *"according to"* "B." Thus, the New Testament believer is *"chosen"* (elected) once he/she is placed into Jesus, the *"chosen* [elect] *one"* of Luke 9:35 and Isaiah 42:1, <u>after</u> repenting and exercising faith while depraved. To what are New Testament believers elected (chosen)? They are elected (chosen) to serve in a special position (office) within the body of Christ. This Scripturally sound interpretation allows God's *"foreknowledge"* ("B") to precede that time when the

New Testament believer is *"chosen"* or elected ("A") to office (reference Diagrams 2 and 8). Thus, we were not elected (chosen) from eternity past to one day be saved/justified. Like Romans 9:11 and 11:5, these verses (1Peter 1:1-2) are addressed in more depth in *God's Heart as it Relates to Election/Atonement/Grace/Perseverance*, the fourth book of this *God's Heart* series.

It would serve you well (when time permits) to look up every instance where *"according to"* is used in the Scriptures. You will find the consistency of God's Word amazing.

This completes our study of **The Contextual View Of *"Predestined"*** and **The Awesomeness of *"According To."*** We will next evaluate how Calvinism and Arminianism perceive predestination by examining the writings of some of their more notable followers. We can then comprehend **The Opposing Views, And How They Came Into Existence**. Such an analysis will reveal why they reject **The Contextual View Of *"Predestined."*** We are steadily progressing through the following outline:

Outline Revisited

I.   **The Contextual View Of *"Predestined"*** (Acts 4:28; 1Corinthians 2:7; Romans 8:29; Romans 8:30; Ephesians 1:5; Ephesians 1:11)

II.   **The Awesomeness of *"According To"***

III.   **The Opposing Views, And How They Came Into Existence**

IV.   **The TULIP: Hyper, Extreme, And Moderate Calvinism's General Views**

V.   **How Arminianism Generally Views The TULIP**

VI.   **A Summary Of Discoveries Regarding The Term *"Predestined"***

Sovereignty, depravity, faith, election, the believer's chosenness, faith followed by regeneration or regeneration followed by faith, free will, limited atonement versus unlimited atonement, and other subjects will be mentioned only briefly in the remainder of this section but are covered in greater detail in other portions of the *God's Heart* series. Consequently, the majority of your questions relating to these highly debated topics will eventually be addressed. These subjects are extremely interwoven, so to tackle them all at the same time would be ill-advised. Patience is the name of the game in all areas of Biblical study, especially the present one.

CHAPTER NINE

III. THE OPPOSING VIEWS, AND HOW THEY CAME INTO EXISTENCE

TO DESCRIBE IN DETAIL WHAT ALL CALVINISTS BELIEVE is no possible. But, the three main branches of Calvinism—hyper, extreme, and moderate (as I have labeled them)—all view God as having predestined the elect to salvation (from eternity past) by means of an eternal decree. One of their main differences, however, lies in how God deals with the "non-elect"—individuals who die unsaved, or lost. These differences are not minor. In fact, they serve as an extreme source of contention among the three branches.

Arminianism, which also perceives God as having predestined the elect to salvation (from eternity past) by means of an eternal decree, is also addressed in this chapter.

Note the following, realizing that Reformed Theology is extreme and hyper Calvinism. Be sure to take advantage of Diagrams 10 and 11 in the Reference Section.

Hyper-Calvinism

One branch of Calvinism, hyper-Calvinism, perceives God as having predestined the elect (as they define the elect) to salvation and the non-elect (as they define the non-elect) to damnation from eternity past by means of an eternal decree. (The name hyper-Calvinism is offensive to some Calvinists but will be used strictly for the sake of distinguishing between the different views.) This belief stems from their improper view of depravity, which prevents them from perceiving man as capable of choosing Christ prior to spiritual regeneration. As a result, they view God as spiritually regenerating the elect (to bring them out of their depravity) and giving them repentance and faith <u>before</u> they can repent, believe, and be saved. (Reference Diagrams 10 and 11.)

Extreme Calvinism

Another branch of Calvinism, labeled by some as extreme Calvinism, holds basically the same view of predestination as the hyper-Calvinists—with one variation (in their minds at least). Instead of viewing God as having predestined the non-elect to damnation from eternity past, they perceive Him as having passed over the non-elect, leaving them to the consequence of their sin. Yet, no difference exists between this idea and what the hyper-Calvinists believe, especially since (according to extreme Calvinism) those who have been left to the consequence of their sin cannot believe due to being part of the non-elect. Thus, extreme and hyper-Calvinists, although they would not admit it, have the same basic view of predestination. We will address this issue in more detail as we progress. (Reference Diagrams 10 and 11.)

Moderate Calvinism

Another branch of Calvinism, moderate Calvinism, views God as having predestined the elect (as they define the "elect") to salvation from eternity past by means of an eternal decree. The non-elect, according to this view, have not been predestined to damnation. The moderate Calvinists also, in most cases, view man as having no need to be spiritually regenerated prior to making a choice to believe (unlike the extreme and hyper-Calvinists). In other words, they view the depraved as possessing a free will to exercise their own personal repentance and faith. What is the difference, however, in God predestining (from eternity past) both the elect and the non-elect to their respective eternal destinies versus predestining the elect alone? In both cases, it would be God Who determines the ultimate destiny of both groups of individuals. How so? Even in the case of moderate Calvinism, should the elect have been predestined to salvation from eternity past, the destiny of the non-elect would have been determined by default, even with man possessing a free will to repent and believe while depraved. At least the hyper-Calvinists are willing to admit what many moderate Calvinists won't—that, according to their school of thought, God alone (independent of a choice on man's part) determines who will or won't be saved. Consequently, the free will of man (accepted by most moderate Calvinists) makes no difference in the final outcome—for they (the moderate Calvinists) perceive the elect as incapable of dying unsaved. They also deem it impossible for the non-elect to choose to believe (although they might struggle to admit this critical fact). Therefore, the moderate Calvinists view only the elect as having been predestined from eternity past (by means of an eternal decree), unlike the hyper-Calvinists. Yet, this false assumption leaves no room for their view of free will to impact the destiny of either the elect or the non-elect because God ultimately, within moderate Calvinism, makes the choice from eternity past. Do you see the contradiction? Keep this in mind as we continue. (Reference Diagrams 10 and 11.)

Arminianism

Arminius believed that God (from eternity past) looked into the future and, by means of His eternal foreknowledge, saw who would repent and believe while depraved. God then, based on his (Arminius') theology, elected (chose) and predestined these future believers to salvation from eternity past by means of an eternal decree (reference Diagrams 4 and 5). Arminianism came into existence when James Arminius, who previously followed Calvinism, rejected the extremes of Calvinism.

The Pitfalls of Isolating Verses

We should forever be aware of the fact that one verse of Scripture, or group of Scriptures, taken out of context, is incapable of sustaining a system of thought. For instance, Paul stated to the church at Rome:

> *But I am speaking to you who are Gentiles. Inasmuch then as I am*
> *an apostle of Gentiles, I magnify my ministry, if somehow I might*
> *move to jealousy my fellow countrymen and save some of them.*
> (Romans 11:13-14)

If this verse were the lone verse that dealt with the salvation of the believer, we might conclude that Paul possessed the power to save the lost. However, the book of Acts repudiates such thinking:

> *And there is salvation in no one else; for there is no other name*
> *under heaven that has been given among men, by which we must be*
> *saved.* (Acts 4:12)

Acts 4:12 refers to Jesus Christ, Who alone can save.

Another example of the importance of studying verses in their context is Romans 10:5:

> *For Moses writes that the man who practices the righteousness*
> *which is based on law shall live by that righteousness.* (Romans
> 10:5)

Is Paul teaching that man can obtain a righteous standing before God through keeping the Law? That idea, on the surface at least, might appear to be true. However, the previous verse, Romans 10:4, disproves it:

> *For Christ is the end of the law for righteousness to everyone who*
> *believes.* (Romans 10:4)

In Romans 9:31-32a we also find:

> *but Israel, pursuing a law of righteousness, did not arrive at that*
> *law. Why? Because they did not pursue it by faith, but as though it*
> *were by works....* (Romans 9:31-32a)

Thus, Romans 10:5 cannot possibly teach that righteousness is obtained through the works of the Law. Instead, Romans 10:5 is saying that those who attempt to work their way into a righteous standing with God will be required to keep the Law perfectly—a total impossibility based on James 2:10 and Romans 3:23:

> *For whoever keeps the whole law and yet stumbles in one point, he*
> *has become guilty of all.* (James 2:10)

> *for all have sinned and fall short of the glory of God,* (Romans
> 3:23)

Our conclusion is also confirmed by verses such as Romans 3:20, Romans 5:20, Galatians 3:24, and 1Timothy 1:9-10. Thus, building any system of thought on isolated passages is unwise.

Calvinists and their Contradictions

We must never assume that anything taught by man is truth until it is tested against every word, phrase, verse, chapter, and book in God's Word. We have attempted to honor this principle up to now, and we will strive to continue on this same path to the end. Many stumbling blocks can be avoided by remaining true to the full counsel of God's Word—every word, phrase, verse, chapter, and book. Sadly, Calvinists such as Edwin H. Palmer ignore the full counsel, as is confirmed by his work, *The Five Points of Calvinism,* pages 85-87. Remember that wording is sometimes inserted between brackets [ ] for clarification and underlines for emphasis:

> ...the Calvinist accepts both sides of the antinomy [an "antinomy" is two truths that contradict each other, which is impossible, but something that the Calvinist must accept]. He realizes that what he advocates is ridiculous. It is simply impossible for man to harmonize these two sets of data. To say on the one hand that God has made certain all that ever happens, and yet to say that man is responsible for what he does? Nonsense! It must be one or the other, but not both. To say that God foreordains the sin of Judas, and yet Judas is to blame? Foolishness!...
>
> This is in accord with Paul, who said, "The word of the cross is to them that perish foolishness" (1Cor. 1:18). The Greeks seek after wisdom and logic, and to them the Calvinist is irrational. <u>The Calvinist holds to two apparently contradictory positions.</u>
>
> So the Calvinist has to make up his mind: what is his authority? His own human reason or the Word of God?
>
> If he answers, the human reasoning powers, then, like the Arminian and hyper-Calvinist, he will have to exclude one of the two parallel forces. But he cannot do that, for he believes the Bible is God's Word and that it was inspired by the Holy Spirit. He trusts God entirely, knowing that His Word cannot be broken. It is infallible and inerrant.
>
> With that firm belief and a willingness to believe everything in it, he accepts this paradox of divine sovereignty and human responsibility. <u>He cannot reconcile the two, but seeing that the Bible clearly teaches both, he accepts both....</u>
>
> The Calvinist's motto is Deuteronomy 29:29, where Moses says that "the secret things belong to the Lord our God; but the things that are revealed belong to us and to our children forever, that we may do all the words of the law." There are certain matters that are

> too deep for man. He cannot and never will comprehend them. He is finite and God is infinite. One of these matters is the apparent paradox of the sovereignty of God and the responsibility of man. This secret matter belongs to the Lord our God, and we should leave it there. We ought not to probe into that secret counsel of God.[42]

In case you wonder what influenced Palmer, read the following quote form Calvin's *Institutes*:

> To many this seems a perplexing subject, because they deem it most incongruous that of the great body of mankind some should be predestinated to salvation, and others to destruction. (*Institutes*: Book 3; Chapter 21; Section 1)[43]

> The decree, I admit, is, dreadful; and yet it is impossible to deny that God foreknew what the end of man was to be before he made him, and foreknew, because he had so ordained by his decree....Nor ought it to seem absurd when I say, that God not only foresaw the fall of the first man, and in him the ruin of his posterity; but also at his own pleasure arranged it. For as it belongs to his wisdom to foreknow all future events, so it belongs to his power to rule and govern them by his hand. (*Institutes*: Book 3; Chapter 23; Section 7)[44]

This "decree" is truly "dreadful" (to use Calvin's words) should what Palmer states below be correct:

> Foreordination means God's sovereign plan, whereby He decides all that is to happen in the entire universe. Nothing in this world happens by chance. God is in back of everything. He decides and causes all things to happen that do happen....He has foreordained everything, "after the counsel of his will" (Ephesians 1:11): the moving of a finger, the beating of a heart, the laughter of a girl, the mistake of a typist—even sin. (*The Five Points of Calvinism*, pages 24-25)[45]

If this description correctly portrays the God of the Bible, no wonder so many theists have cursed Him and walked away.

We must ask ourselves a serious question. Does a contradiction exist between the sovereignty of God and the free will of man? Of course not, that is unless one makes God the cause of all things, as do many Calvinists (especially the extreme and hyper-Calvinists—Reformed theologians). However, if God is <u>not</u> the cause of all things, man can possess a free will (even a free will to repent and believe while depraved) and God remain sovereign. In fact, the reality that God fulfills His prophecies without removing the free will of man makes Him much larger (and much more sovereign) than a "God" who causes man's every action.

The Answer to the Dilemma

The answer to the "dilemma" that so permeates Arminianism and Calvinism is obvious. Their failure to make a distinction between the blessings associated with salvation and salvation itself is their Achilles heel. This flaw has forced them to generate a wealth of materials in their attempt to explain the contradictions that so inundate their polarized systems of thought.

Page after page of ideas, notions, concepts, and illogical thinking within Calvinism never answer the ultimate question: If God is capable of saving all, yet determined from eternity past who will be saved (Calvinism's view), how can He be a God of love having chosen to save so few? R.C. Sproul, an outspoken advocate of Reformed Theology, writes the following in response to this question in *Chosen by God,* pages 36-37:

> The question remains. Why does God only save some? If we grant that God can save men by violating their wills, why then does he not violate everybody's will and bring them all to salvation?...

> The only answer I can give to this question is that I don't know. I have no idea why God saves some but not all. I don't doubt for a moment that God has the power to save all, but I know that he does not choose to save all. I don't know why.[46]

I appreciate Sproul's honesty, but the answer to the dilemma presented by Calvinism is very simple: (1) Recognize that the depraved possess the freedom to repent and believe (2) Understand that New Testament believers are predestined (once they repent and believe while depraved and are made new in Christ) to blessings associated with salvation rather than predestined to salvation from eternity past. This correction in thinking allows man's ultimate destiny to be determined by man's choice (not by God's choice), leaving God capable of saving all (and at the same time desiring that all be saved—1 Timothy 2:4; 2 Peter 3:9), but only saving some. Calvinists, especially Reformed theologians, would say that man choosing his destiny, rather than God making that decision from eternity past, would make God less sovereign and, therefore, subject to the will of man. Th[...]

idea would <u>not</u> be true if, within the realm of His sovereignty, and without predestining a single person to salvation from eternity past by means of an eternal decree, He freely willed that the depraved can choose to repent and believe. Accepting this remedy would eliminate Calvinism, so the disparity continues. Sproul goes on to say:

> One thing I do know. If it pleases God to save some and not all, there is nothing wrong with that.[47]

I disagree. Something is severely wrong with God saving some instead of all if God determined from eternity past (by means of an eternal decree) who will or won't be saved. How can He remain a God of love (1John 4:8, 16) if He elected (according to Calvinism's definition of election) some when He could have elected all? If He could have chosen to save all (as Calvinists believe), but only "chose" to save some (as Calvinists also believe), He cannot possibly be the loving God displayed so vibrantly in His letter to man. What then is their answer? Sproul, sidestepping the issue, writes:

> God is not under obligation to save anyone. If he chooses to save some, that in no way obligates him to save the rest.[48]

Sproul is right in that "God is <u>not</u> under obligation to save anyone." All mankind is deserving of God's wrath. But his statement, "If he chooses to save some, that in no way obligates him to save the rest," is valid only if: (1) God does not possess the power to save all (which He does) (2) God does not desire that all (every human being) be saved (which He does—1Timothy 2:4; 2Peter 3:9) (3) God is not a God of love (which He is—1John 4:8, 16).

Because God possesses the power to save all, desires that all be saved, and truly is a God of love, He would be delighted to save all if it were His choice (and not man's) that determines where man will spend eternity. Due to a misunderstanding of depravity, a subject addressed in much depth in *God's Heart as it Relates to Depravity* (the third book of this *God's Heart* series), Sproul and other Calvinists view unregenerate man as incapable of choosing Christ. Thus, according to their system of thought, God was required to do the choosing from eternity past. This theory generates a contradiction of such magnitude that the followers of this error normally: (1) classify the contradiction as "mystery" and accept it as fact (2) admit that it can't be reconciled, declaring ignorance (3) attack those who would hold them accountable to resolving the contradiction by means of the Scriptures interpreted in context (4) or walk away from Calvinism altogether.

Calvin and Ignorance

Calvin attempted to reconcile his view of predestination by yielding to ignorance:

> Let it, therefore, be our first principle that to desire any other
> knowledge of <u>predestination</u> than that which is expounded by the
> word of God, is no less infatuated than to walk where there is no
> path, or to seek light in darkness. <u>Let us not be ashamed to be</u>
> <u>ignorant in a matter in which ignorance is learning.</u> <u>Rather let us</u>
> <u>willingly abstain from the search after knowledge, to which it is</u>
> <u>both foolish as well as perilous, and even fatal to aspire.</u> (*Institutes*:
> Book 3; Chapter 21; Section 2)[49]

That Calvin viewed ignorance as the solution to the plethora of contradictions generated by his illogical ideology is hard to believe. Yet, he viewed predestination, based on his definition of the term, as "that which is expounded by the word of God." No wonder so many sincere hearts are confused over the topic of predestination.

Consider the following from Calvin as he <u>attempts</u> to defend his view of predestination against those in opposition:

> These observations would be amply sufficient for the pious and
> modest, and such as remember that they are men. But because
> many are the species of blasphemy which these virulent dogs utter
> against God, we shall, as far as the case admits, give an answer to
> each. Foolish men raise many grounds of quarrel with God, as if
> they held him subject to their accusations. First, they ask why God
> is offended with his creatures <u>who have not provoked him by any</u>
> <u>previous offense;</u> for <u>to devote to destruction whomsoever he</u>
> <u>pleases,</u> more resembles the caprice of a tyrant than the legal
> sentence of a judge; and, therefore, there is reason to expostulate
> with God, if at his mere pleasure men are, without any desert of
> their own, <u>predestinated to eternal death.</u> If at any time thoughts of
> this kind come into the minds of the pious, they will be sufficiently
> armed to repress them, by considering how sinful it is to insist on
> knowing the causes of the divine will, since it is itself, and justly
> ought to be, the cause of all that exists....The will of God is the
> supreme rule of righteousness, so that everything which he wills
> must be held to be righteous by the mere fact of his willing it.
> Therefore, when it is asked why the Lord did so, we must answer,
> Because he pleased. But if you proceed farther to ask why he

pleased, you ask for something greater and more sublime than the will of God, and nothing such can be found. Let human temerity then be quiet, and cease to inquire after what exists not, lest perhaps it fails to find what does exist. This, I say, will be sufficient to restrain any one who would reverently contemplate the secret things of God. Against the audacity of the wicked, who hesitate not openly to blaspheme, God will sufficiently defend himself by his own righteousness, without our assistance, when depriving their consciences of all means of evasion, he shall hold them under conviction, and make them feel their guilt. We, however, give no countenance to the fiction of absolute power, which, as it is heathenish, so it ought justly to be held in detestation by us. We do not imagine God to be lawless. He is a law to himself; because, as Plato says, men laboring under the influence of concupiscence need law; but the will of God is not only free from all vice, but is the supreme standard of perfection, the law of all laws. But we deny that he is bound to give an account of his procedure; and we moreover deny that we are fit of our own ability to give judgment in such a case. Wherefore, when we are tempted to go farther than we ought, let this consideration deter us, Thou shalt be "justified when thou speakest, and be clear when thou judges," (Psa 51: 4). (*Institutes*: Book 3; Chapter 23; Section 2)[50]

Note that Calvin fails to resolve the many contradictions his ideology generates, one of which is: God predestines certain persons to damnation "who have not provoked him by any previous offense." Instead of presenting a non-contradictory answer, Calvin not only ridicules those who take issue with his dogma, but places predestination in the category of the secret things of God. Why? Non-contradictory answers to the inconsistencies within Calvinism do not exist. Consequently, Calvin's view of predestination (as it relates to the elect as well as the non-elect) is unbiblical.

John MacArthur's words from *The MacArthur New Testament Commentary, Ephesians*, page 11, are amazingly similar to those of Calvin:

God's sovereign election and man's exercise of responsibility in choosing Jesus Christ seem opposite and irreconcilable truths—and from our limited human perspective they *are* opposite and irreconcilable. That is why so many earnest, well-meaning Christians throughout the history of the church have floundered trying to reconcile them. Since the problem cannot be resolved by our finite minds, the result is always to compromise one truth in favor of the other or to weaken both by trying to take a position

> somewhere between them. We should let the antinomy remain,
> believing both truths completely and leaving the harmonizing of
> them to God.[51]

I totally disagree with these conclusions, as the body of this work verifies.

Not Superior Thinkers

Considering the previous quotes from Calvin and MacArthur, ponder R.C. Sproul's words from *Chosen by God*, page 15. Words included in brackets [ ] are inserted for clarification.

> Those thinkers who are most widely regarded as the titans of
> classical Christian scholarship fall heavily on the Reformed side. I
> am persuaded, however, that this is a fact of history that dare not be
> ignored....we must take seriously the fact that such learned men
> agreed on this difficult subject [the subject of predestination].
> Again, that they agreed does not prove the case for predestination.
> They could have been wrong. But it gets our attention.[52]

A question that must be asked is: "Who was responsible for concluding that those on the Reformed side, the side of extreme and hyper-Calvinism, have been, and are, generally the most scholarly?" If these "thinkers" could develop a belief system containing such irreconcilable ambiguities, maybe it is time to rethink that classification. Calvin, evidently, had a brilliant mind in the realm of the natural. In the opinion of some theologians, however, he was deficient in the area of sound Biblical exegesis. Spiritual maturity is not dependent on intellectual aptitude (Acts 4:13; 1Corinthians 1:26-29). It results from a proper understanding of God's heart! As a consequence of Calvin's distorted view of predestination, God's heart was misinterpreted and, therefore, grossly misrepresented. Who influenced Calvin's perception of predestination? The following is almost impossible to believe.

Augustine's Influence on Calvin

Calvin, who is known as one of the Reformers, actually obtained his view of predestination from Augustine, the most influential leader in the history of the Catholic Church. Note the following quote from Augustine's, *On the Soul and its Origin* (Book 4; Chapter 16):

> That owing to one man all pass into condemnation who are born of
> Adam unless they are born again in Christ, even as He has
> appointed them to be regenerated, before they die in the body,
> whom He <u>predestined to everlasting life</u>, as the most merciful
> bestower of grace; while to those whom He has <u>predestined to
> eternal death</u>, He is also the most righteous awarder of punishment
> not only on account of the sins which they add in the indulgence of
> their own will, but also because of their original sin, even if, as in
> the case of infants, they add nothing thereto.[53]

Augustine, who early in his ministry viewed the depraved as possessing a free
will to repent and believe, changed his theological position (review the chart at the
end of Chapter Five). Later in his ministry, in fact, he discarded his view of free
will by perceiving the elect as having been predestined (by God) to salvation from
eternity past (a scenario supported nowhere in the Scriptures). He also believed
that God "predestined" certain persons "to eternal death." Calvin's words, as
quoted from Calvin's, *A Treatise on the Eternal Predestination of God* (trans.
Henry Cole: 38), confirm the degree to which Augustine influenced his thinking:

> In a word, Augustine is so wholly with me, that if I wished to write
> a confession of my faith, I could do so with all fullness and
> satisfaction to myself out of his writings. But that I may not, on the
> present occasion, be too prolix, I will be content with three or four
> instances of his testimony, from which it will be manifest that he
> does not differ from me one pin's point. And it would be more
> manifest still, could the whole line of his confession be adduced,
> how fully and solidly he agrees with me in every particular.[54]

A Closer Look at Calvin's Theology

Calvin possessed a radical view of God's sovereignty and, in turn, a radical view of
predestination—much of which resulted from his exposure to Augustine's writings.
After all, Calvin was raised in the Catholic Church, a church inundated with
Augustinian thought. Note Calvin's words from *Institutes*. (Even if these quotes
initially seem difficult to follow, please take the time to read them in their entirety.
Just comprehend what you can and leave the remainder for another day. It may
become obvious as to why some Calvinists attempt to separate themselves from
Calvin.)

The covenant of life is not preached equally to all, and among those to whom it is preached, does not always meet with the same reception. This diversity displays the unsearchable depth of the divine judgment, and is without doubt subordinate to God's purpose of eternal election. But if it is plainly owing to the mere pleasure of God that salvation is spontaneously offered to some, while others have no access to it, great and difficult questions immediately arise, questions which are inexplicable, when just views are not entertained concerning election and predestination. To many this seems a perplexing subject, because they deem it most incongruous that of the great body of mankind some should be predestinated to salvation, and others to destruction. How ceaselessly they entangle themselves will appear as we proceed. We may add, that in the very obscurity which deters them, we may see not only the utility of this doctrine, but also its most pleasant fruits. We shall never feel persuaded as we ought that our salvation flows from the free mercy of God as its fountain, until we are made acquainted with his eternal election, the grace of God being illustrated by the contrast, viz., that he does not adopt all promiscuously to the hope of salvation, but gives to some what he denies to others. It is plain how greatly ignorance of this principle detracts from the glory of God, and impairs true humility. (*Institutes*: Book 3; Chapter 21; Section 1)[55]

I admit that profane men lay hold of the subject of predestination to carp, or cavil, or snarl, or scoff. But if their petulance frightens us, it will be necessary to conceal all the principal articles of faith, because they and their fellows leave scarcely one of them unassailed with blasphemy.... Those, however, who are so cautious and timid, that they would bury all mention of predestination in order that it may not trouble weak minds, with what color, pray, will they cloak their arrogance, when they indirectly charge God with a want of due consideration, in not having foreseen a danger for which they imagine that they prudently provide? Whoever, therefore, throws obloquy on the doctrine of predestination, openly brings a charge against God, as having inconsiderately allowed something to escape from him which is injurious to the Church. (*Institutes*: Book 3; Chapter 21; Section 4)[56]

The human mind, when it hears this doctrine, cannot restrain its petulance, but boils and rages as if aroused by the sound of a trumpet. Many professing a desire to defend the Deity from an invidious charge admit the doctrine of election, but deny that any one is reprobated, (Bernard. in Die Ascensionis, Serm. 2). This they do ignorantly and childishly since there could be no election without its opposite reprobation. God is said to set apart those whom he adopts for salvation. It were most absurd to say, that he admits others fortuitously, or that they by their industry acquire what election alone confers on a few. Those, therefore, whom God passes by he reprobates, and that for no other cause but because he is pleased to exclude them from the inheritance which he predestines to his children. (*Institutes*: Book 3; Chapter 23; Section 1)[57]

But if all whom the Lord predestines to death are naturally liable to sentence of death, of what injustice, pray, do they complain? Should all the sons of Adam come to dispute and contend with their Creator, because by his eternal providence they were before their birth doomed to perpetual destruction, when God comes to reckon with them, what will they be able to mutter against this defense? If all are taken from a corrupt mass, it is not strange that all are subject to condemnation. Let them not, therefore, charge God with injustice, if by his eternal judgment they are doomed to a death to which they themselves feel that whether they will or not they are drawn spontaneously by their own nature. Hence it appears how perverse is this affectation of murmuring, when of set purpose they suppress the cause of condemnation which they are compelled to recognize in themselves, that they may lay the blame upon God. (*Institutes*: Book 3; Chapter 23; Section 3)[58]

First, all must admit what Solomon says, "The Lord has made all things for himself; yea, even the wicked for the day of evil," (Pro 16: 4). Now, since the arrangement of all things is in the hand of God, since to him belongs the disposal of life and death, he arranges all things by his sovereign counsel, in such a way that individuals are born, who are doomed from the womb to certain death, and are to glorify him by their destruction. (*Institutes*: Book 3; Chapter 23; Section 6)[59]

God, according to the good pleasure of his will, without any regard to merit, elects those whom he chooses for sons, while he rejects and reprobates others. ... It is asked, how it happens that of two, between whom there is no difference of merit, God in his election adopts the one, and passes by the other? I, in my turn, ask, Is there any thing in him who is adopted to incline God towards him? If it must be confessed that there is nothing, it will follow, that God looks not to the man, but is influenced entirely by his own goodness to do him good. Therefore, when God elects one and rejects another, it is owing not to any respect to the individual, but entirely to his own mercy which is free to display and exert itself when and where he pleases. (*Institutes*: Book 3; Chapter 23; Section 10)[60]

We say, then, that Scripture clearly proves this much, that God by his eternal and immutable counsel determined once for all those whom it was his pleasure one day to admit to salvation, and those whom, on the other hand, it was his pleasure to doom to destruction. We maintain that this counsel, as regards the elect, is founded on his free mercy, without any respect to human worth, while those whom he dooms to destruction are excluded from access to life by a just and blameless, but at the same time incomprehensible judgment. In regard to the elect, we regard calling as the evidence of election, and justification as another symbol of its manifestation, until it is fully accomplished by the attainment of glory. But as the Lord seals his elect by calling and justification, so by excluding the reprobate either from the knowledge of his name or the sanctification of his Spirit, he by these marks in a manner discloses the judgment which awaits them. (*Institutes*: Book 3; Chapter 21; Section 7)[61]

Interestingly, Calvin seems to believe that Adam possessed a free will based on the following statements:

It were here unseasonable to introduce the question concerning the secret predestination of God, because we are not considering what might or might not happen, but what the nature of man truly was. Adam, therefore, might have stood if he chose, since it was only by his own will that he fell; but it was because his will was pliable in either directions and he had not received constancy to persevere, that he so easily fell. Still he had a free choice of good and evil; and not only so, but in the mind and will there was the highest rectitude, and all the organic parts were duly framed to obedience, until man corrupted its good properties, and destroyed himself. (*Institutes:* Book 1; Chapter 15; Section 8—underline mine)[62]

Calvin seems to contradict these words by scoffing at the idea that Adam possessed a free will:

> They deny that it is ever said in distinct terms, God decreed that
> Adam should perish by his revolt. As if the same God, who is
> declared in Scripture to do whatsoever he pleases, could have made
> the noblest of his creatures without any special purpose. They say
> that, in accordance with free-will, he was to be the architect of his
> own fortune, that God had decreed nothing but to treat him
> according to his desert. If this frigid fiction is received, where will
> be the omnipotence of God, by which, according to his secret
> counsel on which every thing depends, he rules over all? ... I again
> ask how it is that the fall of Adam involves so many nations with
> their infant children in eternal death without remedy unless that it
> so seemed meet to God? Here the most loquacious tongues must be
> dumb. The decree, I admit, is, dreadful; and yet it is impossible to
> deny that God foreknow what the end of man was to be before he
> made him, and foreknew, because he had so ordained by his
> decree. Should any one here inveigh against the prescience of God,
> he does it rashly and unadvisedly. For why, pray, should it be made
> a charge against the heavenly Judge, that he was not ignorant of
> what was to happen? Thus, if there is any just or plausible
> complaint, it must be directed against predestination. Nor ought it
> to seem absurd when I say, that God not only foresaw the fall of
> the first man, and in him the ruin of his posterity; but also at his
> own pleasure arranged it. For as it belongs to his wisdom to
> foreknow all future events, so it belongs to his power to rule and
> govern them by his hand. (*Institutes*—Book 3; Chapter 23; Section
> 7)[63]

Thus, Calvin believed that God asked Adam to abstain from eating of the tree of
the knowledge of good and evil so He could punish Adam for his disobedience, a
disobedience that God had predestined from eternity past. Note once more Calvin's
words:

> The first man fell because the Lord deemed it meet that he should:
> why he deemed it meet, we know not. It is certain, however, that it
> was just, because he saw that his own glory would thereby be
> displayed. When you hear the glory of God mentioned, understand
> that his justice is included. For that which deserves praise must be
> just. Man therefore falls, divine providence so ordaining, but he
> falls by his own fault. The Lord had a little before declared that all
> the things which he had made were very good, (Gen 1: 31).
> Whence then the depravity of man, which made him revolt from
> God? Lest it should be supposed that it was from his creation, God

135

had expressly approved what proceeded from himself. Therefore man's own wickedness corrupted the pure nature which he had received from God, and his ruin brought with it the destruction of all his posterity. Wherefore, let us in the corruption of human nature contemplate the evident cause of condemnation, (a cause which comes more closely home to us), rather than inquire into a cause hidden and almost incomprehensible in the <u>predestination</u> of God. Nor let us decline to submit our judgment to the boundless wisdom of God, so far as to confess its insufficiency to comprehend many of his secrets. <u>Ignorance of things which we are not able, or which it is not lawful to know, is learning, while the desire to know them is a species of madness.</u> (*Institutes*: Book 3; Chapter 23; Section 8—underline mine)[64]

Is this the God of the Scriptures? We would need to cease reasoning to accept such a mindset! Of course, such a state of non-thinking is what Calvin prescribed in the first place, but attempted to cover up. Note Calvin's words:

If we give due weight to the consideration, that the word of the Lord is the only way which can conduct us to the investigation of whatever it is lawful for us to hold with regard to him - is the only light which can enable us to discern what we ought to see with regard to him, it will curb and restrain all presumption. For it will show us that the moment we go beyond the bounds of the word we are out of the course, in darkness, and must every now and then stumble, go astray, and fall. Let it, therefore, be our first principle that to desire any other knowledge of <u>predestination</u> than that which is expounded by the word of God, is no less infatuated than to walk where there is no path, or to seek light in darkness. <u>Let us not be ashamed to be ignorant in a matter in which ignorance is learning. Rather let us willingly abstain from the search after knowledge, to which it is both foolish as well as perilous, and even fatal to aspire.</u> If an unrestrained imagination urges us, our proper course is to oppose it with these words, "It is not good to eat much honey: so for men to search their own glory is not glory," (Pro 25: 27). There is good reason to dread a presumption which can only plunge us headlong into ruin. (*Institutes*: Book 3; Chapter 21; Section 2—underline mine)[65]

Everything, therefore delivered in Scripture on the subject of <u>predestination</u>, we must beware of keeping from the faithful, lest we seem either maliciously to deprive them of the blessing of God,

> or to accuse and scoff at the Spirit, as having divulged what ought
> on any account to be suppressed. Let us, I say, allow the Christian
> to unlock his mind and ears to all the words of God which are
> addressed to him, provided he do it with this moderation, viz., that
> whenever the Lord shuts his sacred mouth, he also desists from
> inquiry. The best rule of sobriety is, not only in learning to follow
> wherever God leads, but also when he makes an end of teaching, to
> cease also from wishing to be wise. The danger which they dread is
> not so great that we ought on account of it to turn away our minds
> from the oracles of God. There is a celebrated saying of Solomon,
> "It is the glory of God to conceal a thing," (Pro 25: 2). But since
> both piety and common sense dictate that this is not to be
> understood of every thing, we must look for a distinction, lest
> under the pretence of modesty and sobriety we be satisfied with a
> brutish ignorance. (*Institutes*: Book 3; Chapter 21; Section 3)[66]

How can this reasoning be viewed as Scriptural when 1Peter 3:15 clearly states:

> *...always being ready to make a defense to everyone who asks you*
> *to give an account for the hope that is in you....* (1Peter 3:15)

Who would accept a defense inundated with contradictory testimony? Courts of Law are established to make certain that the accused are convicted or set free based on the truth, ensuring that every contradictory statement is totally nullified. Are we not to expect God's Word, written by the righteous Judge of the universe, to be free of contradiction from beginning to end?   Is God so incapably of properly expressing Himself that we must yield to "mystery" in an attempt to cover His inadequacies? Never!

These thoughts bring to mind the justice of God.   How could He have predestined the lost to hell from eternity past (by means of an eternal decree), judge them for not believing, and remain just? Mystery is often cited (or implied) by the Calvinist, even by Calvin himself, while attempting to explain the obvious contradiction:

> The reprobate [those predestined to damnation] would excuse their
> sins by alleging that they are unable to escape the necessity of
> sinning, especially because a necessity of this nature is laid upon
> them by the <u>ordination</u> of God. We deny that they can thus be
> validly excused, since the <u>ordination</u> of God, by which they
> complain that they are doomed to destruction, is consistent with
> equity, an equity, indeed, <u>unknown to us</u> [mystery, I guess], <u>but</u>
> <u>most certain</u>. Hence we conclude, that every evil which they bear is

> inflicted by the most just judgment of God. (*Institutes*: Book 3; Chapter 23; Section 9)[67]

Calvin attempted to defend his view of the justice of God by claiming that everything He wills is righteous:

> The will of God is the supreme rule of righteousness, so that everything which he wills must be held to be righteous by the mere fact of his willing it. Therefore, when it is asked why the Lord did so, we must answer, Because he pleased. But if you proceed farther to ask why he pleased, you ask for something greater and more sublime than the will of God, and nothing such can be found. Let human temerity then be quiet, and cease to inquire after what exists not, lest perhaps it fails to find what does exist. This, I say, will be sufficient to restrain any one who would reverently contemplate the secret things of God. (*Institutes*: Book 3; Chapter 23; Section 2)[68]

How can everything that God wills be righteous should He will all things, even sin (the bottom line of Reformed Theology—extreme and hyper-Calvinism)? Calvin's God also predestined men to hell by means of an eternal decree, causes them to be born void of an ability to believe, condemns them for failing to believe and remains just solely because everything He wills must be categorized as righteous. No way! Note what John Wesley had to say regarding the subject:

> He [God] will punish no man for doing anything he could not possibly avoid; neither for omitting anything which he could not possibly do. Every punishment supposes the offender might have avoided the offence for which he is punished. Otherwise, to punish him would be palpably unjust, and inconsistent with the character of God...(Laurence M. Vance, *The Other Side of Calvinism*, 236)[69]

Somehow, Calvin's God forces Himself upon the elect (which many Calvinist would struggle to admit), yet remains a God of love. One would have to cease thinking to accept such a mindset.

Dave Hunt (who is not a Calvinist), in his book, *What Love Is This?* (page 426) records James R. White's words (who is a Calvinist) regarding Calvin:

> John Calvin is admitted, even by his foes, to have been a tremendous exegete of Scripture. Fair and insightful, Calvin's commentaries continue to this day to have great usefulness and benefit to the student of Scripture.[70]

Would you agree with White's assessment of Calvin after having read the previous quotes from Calvin's *Institutes?* Your answer would have to be "No!" if you take Calvin's conclusions through the full counsel of God's Word—every word, phrase, verse, chapter, and book.

The Remedy to the Confusion

The good news is that all of this contradiction vanishes when Scripture alone is allowed to rule. When mankind is granted a free will to repent and believe while depraved, with all who choose to accept Christ during the church age being predestined to blessing once they exercise personal repentance and faith, contradiction is nowhere to be found. As was mentioned in the **Introduction** under **Subjects to be Addressed**, **Depravity** #2, the decisive impulse to repent and believe is provided by the depraved. God, however, draws all the depraved (every person) to Himself (John 6:44; 12:32; 16:8), not wishing that any perish (1Timothy 2:4; 2Peter 3:9)—although the majority reject His free offer of grace. Romans 3:27-28 and Romans 4:4-5 also confirm that to exercise faith in one's depravity is not a work.

All Calvinists would disagree with this remedy due to perceiving the "elect" as having been elected and predestined to salvation from eternity past by means of an eternal decree. The extreme and hyper-Calvinists would especially differ, claiming that unregenerate man lacks the ability to turn to the Savior. They adhere to this mindset because of their unhealthy (contradictory) view of depravity, a topic discussed in great depth in *God's Heart as it Relates to Depravity*, the third book of this *God's Heart* series.

"Mystery": An Unacceptable Answer to Contradiction

God's Word, being void of contradiction, is not deficient, flawed, or imperfect. Therefore, Calvinism's employment of "mystery" in an attempt to veil its mishandling of the truth is unacceptable.

No doubt, the *"secret things"* belong to God (Deuteronomy 29:29), which does not mean that God's *"secret things"* are the same as God's *"mystery."* Romans 11:25, 16:25-26, 1Corinthians 2:7, 15:51, Ephesians 3:3, 3:8-10, 6:19, Colossians 1:26, 1:27, and Revelation 17:7 confirm that the word *"mystery"* in the New Testament relates to truth that God is in the process of revealing. Consequently, Calvinism's definition of "mystery" contradicts the Biblical application of the term. Scripture never employs "mystery" as a means to classify contradiction as truth, yet

Calvinistic writings consistently apply "mystery" to their overabundance of theological inconsistencies.

The TULIP of the Synod of Dort

The Synod of Dort (1618-1619) is defined by Calvinists as "a gathering of history's most godly leaders." It was actually a gathering of Calvinists (after John Calvin's death in 1564) that produced the five points of Calvinism: TULIP—"T" Total Depravity; "U" Unconditional Election; "L" Limited Atonement; "I" Irresistible Grace; "P" Perseverance of the Saints. This group was highly influenced by Augustine due to Augustine's influence on Calvin. Those who disagreed with their doctrine were persecuted, many of whom were "Arminians" (followers of James Arminius). One of the documents produced by this Synod was *The Judgment Concerning Devine Predestination.* A portion of Article VI of that work states:

> He [God] graciously softens the hearts of the elect, however
> obstinate, and inclines them to behave; while he leaves the non-
> elect in his just judgment to their own wickedness and obduracy.
> And herein is especially displayed the profound, and merciful, and
> at the same time the righteous discrimination between men, equally
> involved in ruin; or that decree of election and reprobation,
> revealed in the Word of God, which though men of perverse,
> impure and unstable minds wrest to their own destruction, yet to
> holy and pious souls affords unspeakable consolation.[71]

Consider what King James (who gave us the King James Bible in 1611) stated after hearing the conclusions of the Synod. Oh, by the way, King James was anything but a saint:

> This doctrine is so horrible, that I am persuaded, if there were a
> council of unclean spirits assembled in hell, and their prince the
> devil were to [ask] their opinion about the most likely means of
> stirring up the hatred of men against God their Maker; nothing
> could be invented by them that would be more efficacious for this
> purpose, or that could put a greater affront upon God's love for
> mankind than that infamous decree of the late Synod.... (Dave
> Hunt; *What Love Is This?*, page 244)[72]

Because King James sent a delegation to Dort, he knew well the ramifications of what the Synod had determined. No wonder he declared:

> "that infamous decree of the late Synod, and the decision of that detestable formulary, by which the far greater part of the human race are condemned to hell for no other reason, *than the mere will of God, without any regard to sin,* the necessity of sinning, as well as that of being damned, being fastened on them by that great nail of the decree before-mentioned" (Dave Hunt; *What Love Is This?,* page 166)[73]

Obviously, King James (who was not "Arminian") did not agree with the Calvinistic idea that God's grace and love would be brilliantly displayed had He selected a few for salvation when He could have selected all.   Too many discrepancies would need to be accepted to approve of this mindset.   In other words, the Calvinists' patented attempt to justify their ideology (by focusing on the wonder that God would select any) failed to satisfy the King.   Should Calvinism be true, how could God, Who is capable of saving all (according to their view), remain a God of love while selecting so few?   This notion is impossible if He, according to Calvinism, elected and predestined individuals to salvation from eternity past!   Hence, "mystery" has become the catchword for the Calvinists.   Yet, note the 1986 statement from Pope John Paul II regarding Augustine, whose writings (Augustine's writings) highly influenced Calvin:

> Augustine's legacy…is the theological methods to which he remained absolutely faithful…full adherence to the authority of the faith…revealed through Scripture, Tradition and the Church…. Likewise the profound sense of mystery—"for it is better," he exclaims, "to have a faithful ignorance than a presumptuous knowledge…." I express once again my fervent desire…that the authoritative teaching of such a great doctor and pastor may flourish ever more happily in the Church….[74]

Augustine's Infamous Doctrines

Augustine's influence on Calvin was enormous. Yet, Augustine is responsible for a variety of dogmas within the Catholic Church, some of which are listed below:

(1)   The allegorical (instead of the literal) interpretation of the Scriptures
(2)   The rejection of the one thousand year reign of Christ on the earth, with the Church now reigning instead
(3)   Satan is bound during the church age
(4)   Infant baptism for regeneration, with all unbaptized babies excluded from the kingdom

(5)   Salvation through the Catholic Church by means of the sacraments
(6)   Purgatory
(7)   The right to persecute those in disagreement with the Catholic Church
(8)   The Catholic Church alone is the body of Christ
(9)   The Lord's supper is the physical presence of Christ's body and blood
(10) The apostolic succession from Peter, making Peter the first Pope
(11) God is the cause of all things
(12) The predestination of some individuals to salvation and others to damnation
(13) Faith is irresistible and a gift from God
(14) Augustine was one of the first to place tradition on an equal plane with the Scriptures
(15) Baptism is necessary for the remission of sins

No wonder Calvin, highly influenced by Augustine, invested excessive time attempting to explain his contradictory presuppositions. Inconsistency classified as "mystery" is impossible to reconcile, no matter how much is written regarding the subject matter.

Even Luther was greatly influenced by Augustine until he eventually saw the light:

> In the beginning, I devoured Augustine, but when…I knew what justification by faith really was, then it was out with him." (George; *Theology*, page 68)[75]

Evidently Calvin, one of the "great" Reformers, never understood that Augustine rejected the truth of justification by faith alone. What does this say regarding Calvin's ability to discern truth from error? In fact, what does it communicate regarding his spiritual maturity? He may have possessed a brilliant mind in the realm of the natural, but he was certainly lacking in the area of Biblical understanding. For this reason, some Calvinists distance themselves from Calvin, instead, calling themselves "Reformed." However, the Reformed view still considers the elect to have been predestined to salvation from eternity past, by means of an eternal decree—needing to be spiritually regenerated, and given repentance and faith, <u>before</u> they can repent, believe, and be saved. Consequently if someone states that he/she is not a Calvinist, but adheres to the Reformed view he/she still believes that the elect were predestined to salvation from eternity past by means of an eternal decree—a contradiction nowhere supported in the Scriptures. (Review Diagrams 10 and 11 in the Reference Section for more input.)

I have addressed less pertaining to Arminianism than Calvinism because Arminius, although at one time a follower of Calvinism (having studied at Calvin's seminary in Geneva), rejected some of the extreme views of the movement. A validated in our previous study of *Foreknowledge*, I disagree with Arminius' mindset because, even though he perceived the depraved as possessing a free will to repent and believe, he continued to view the believer as having been predestined to salvation from eternity past by means of an eternal decree—a total impossibility. (Reference Diagrams 2, 4, 5, and 7).

Before we advance deeper into our examination of the term "predestined," we need to discuss what the extreme and hyper-Calvinists (Reformed theologians), the moderate Calvinists, and the Arminians believe concerning the TULIP. Many variations exist within each system of thought, but the following communicates what is generally accepted. We can build on what is conveyed here as we progress to other topics included in this series. Consulting the diagrams in the Reference Section will be helpful as we proceed.

B.A.S.I.C. TRAINING

CHAPTER TEN

IV. THE TULIP: HYPER, EXTREME, AND MODERATE CALVINISMS' GENERAL VIEWS

THE FIVE POINTS OF CALVINISM are best described by the acrostic "TULIP."

T   **Total Depravity**
U   **Unconditional Election**
L   **Limited Atonement**
I   **Irresistible Grace**
P   **Perseverance of the Saints**

We will now address how Calvinism views the TULIP.

What the Extreme and Hyper-Calvinists Generally Believe Regarding the TULIP

T---Total Depravity

The extreme and hyper-Calvinists perceive the depraved (the spiritual unregenerated) as totally incapable of choosing Christ due to the depth of their spiritual depravity. They perceive the depraved as spiritual corpses.

144

U—Unconditional Election

The hyper-Calvinists view God as not only having predestined and elected the elect (each individual person) to salvation, but also having predestined the non-elect to damnation—both scenarios occurring from eternity past by means of an eternal decree. The extreme Calvinists view God as having predestined the elect (each individual person) to salvation by means of an eternal decree (from eternity past), but having left the non-elect to the consequence of their sin. In both cases, predestination and election were based on God's choice alone, having nothing to do with the worth (merit) of the individual who was predestined and elected. Thus, their election was unconditional, fulfilling Calvinism's "U" of the TULIP, Unconditional Election.

L—Limited Atonement

Both extreme and hyper-Calvinism view Christ as having died for the elect alone. Therefore, they believe in Limited Atonement. In their minds, Jesus' death secured, purchased, or made certain the salvation of the elect at the cross, providing no benefit whatsoever (in regard to salvation) for the non-elect. They draw this conclusion by using the following <u>flawed</u> argument: Because unregenerate man is born totally depraved, and incapable of choosing Christ, God was required to unconditionally elect (by means of an eternal decree) those who will be saved. Because only the elect receive salvation, Christ died for the elect only. Had Christ died for the non-elect, a portion of His blood would have been wasted.

Can you detect the surplus of errors in the previous argument? Extreme and hyper-Calvinists have a limited view of Christ's atoning work due to an incorrect perception of what the cross accomplished. In their minds, only two options exist regarding atonement: (1) Christ died to <u>secure</u> the salvation of the elect only (2) Christ died to <u>secure</u> the salvation of all mankind. Thus, from their perspective, if you do not believe that Christ died for the elect alone (and thus believe in <u>Limited</u> Atonement), you must believe in universalism (the salvation of all mankind). Actually, a non-contradictory view of <u>unlimited</u> atonement exists and will be addressed later.

I—Irresistible Grace

The extreme and hyper-Calvinists perceive the elect as incapable of resisting God's grace. Thus, they adhere to Irresistible Grace. This belief is due to their unhealthy view of depravity, which prevents unregenerate man from possessing the ability to repent and believe. Consequently, according to their way of thinking, God must spiritually regenerate the elect <u>before</u> they can exercise repentance and faith—repentance and faith, according to their view, being God's gifts to the elect subsequent to spiritual regeneration. In other words, repentance and faith follow spiritual regeneration in this arrangement—differing from the Scriptural view which has repentance and faith <u>preceding</u> spiritual regeneration (salvation/justification). Thus, based on extreme and hyper-Calvinism's theology, the grace that God supplies in bringing about this transformation must be irresistible.

P—Perseverance of the Saints

To the extreme and hyper-Calvinists, the proof of election is normally dependent on the perseverance of the elect. Many times, the elect who do not persevere are viewed as part of the non-elect. Consequently, the elect, according to their reasoning, are responsible for completing their salvation (that is, if the extreme and hyper-Calvinists are held accountable to the "bottom button" of what they believe).

What the Moderate Calvinists Generally Believe Regarding the TULIP

T—Total Depravity

Moderate Calvinists normally perceive the depraved (the spiritually unregenerated) as possessing a free will and, therefore, capable of choosing Christ—but not without being drawn by the Father.

U—Unconditional Election

Moderate Calvinists normally view God as having predestined and elected the elect (each individual person) to salvation by means of an eternal decree (from eternity past), without having based their predestination and election on anything other than His choice of them. The moderate Calvinists, therefore, believe in Unconditional Election. They generally, unlike the extreme and hyper-Calvinists, perceive the depraved as capable of exercising repentance and faith. Thus, they usually view man as possessing a free will that allows man to repent and believe <u>prior</u> to being spiritually regenerated. Dr. Norm Geisler (a moderate Calvinist states, in *Chosen But Free*, page 120:

God's Heart   *Predestination, Chapter Ten*

> Unconditional election…is unconditional from the standpoint of
> the Giver, even though there is one condition for the receiver—
> faith.[76]

L—Limited Atonement

In most cases, the moderate Calvinists do <u>not</u> believe in Limited Atonement in the same sense as the Reformed theologian, but view Christ as having died for all mankind. They consider Christ's atonement as <u>providing</u> salvation for all but securing salvation for the elect only—once the elect choose to repent and believe while depraved. The study titled, *God's Heart as it Relates to Election/Atonement/Grace/Perseverance* (the fourth book of this *God's Heart* series), addresses this subject in much greater depth. Note the words of Dr. Norm Geisler, a moderate Calvinist, from *Chosen But Free*, page 121. Can you see how my previous comments pertaining to the moderate view line up with his statements?

> Even limited atonement is affirmed by moderate Calvinists in the
> sense that it is limited in its application. That is, <u>although</u>
> <u>redemption was purchased for all and is available to all,</u>
> nonetheless, it will only be applied to those whom God chose from
> all eternity—the elect.[77]

I—Irresistible Grace

The moderate Calvinists believe (in general) in Irresistible Grace, but the flavor is different from that of extreme and hyper-Calvinism (Reformed Theology). Moderate Calvinists normally view repentance and faith as not only springing forth from the depraved, but also <u>preceding</u> spiritual regeneration. This view differs from that of the extreme and hyper-Calvinists, who believe that spiritual regeneration must precede repentance and faith (which, in their minds, are God's gifts) due to perceiving the depraved as unable to believe. Thus, in the Reformed theologian's mind, God must, by Irresistible Grace, bring the elect to Himself if they are to believe. This concept is diametrically opposed to moderate Calvinism. Dr. Norm Geisler (a moderate Calvinist) writes in *Chosen But Free*, page 121:

> Irresistible grace is held by moderate Calvinists. Irresistible grace
> is exercised on all who are willing….That is, anyone who is
> receptive to God's work in his heart will be overwhelmed by His
> grace.[78]

147

In other words, moderate Calvinism normally holds to the mindset that once a depraved individual chooses to repent and believe, God overwhelms him/her "by His grace."

P—Perseverance of the Saints

Instead of believing in the Perseverance of the Saints in the same context as the extreme and hyper-Calvinists, the moderate Calvinists generally believe in eternal security. Thus, they normally view God as responsible for completing the believer's salvation (Philippians 1:6) rather than the believer persevering for God (the view taken by many extreme and hyper-Calvinists). Note Dr. Geisler's quote from page 121 of *Chosen But Free*, Dr. Geisler being a moderate Calvinist:

> Perseverance of the saints, too, is an essential part of moderate Calvinism. It affirms that all regenerate (justified) people eventually will be saved.... [79]

CHAPTER ELEVEN

V. HOW ARMINIANS GENERALLY VIEW THE TULIP

ARMINIANISM DIFFERS GREATLY FROM CALVINISM. Below is a description of what Arminians <u>generally</u> believe regarding each letter of the acrostic, TULIP.

T—Total Depravity

Arminians view Adam's sin as polluting man, but not severely enough that the depraved (the spiritually unregenerated) cannot choose, as a result of their free will, to accept Christ.

U—Unconditional Election

Arminians adhere to conditional election rather than Unconditional Election. They teach that God (from eternity past) looked into the future and, by means of His eternal foreknowledge, saw who would repent and believe while depraved. God then, based on their theology, elected (chose) and predestined these future believers to salvation from eternity past by means of an eternal decree (reference Diagrams 4 and 5). Consequently, because election (as defined by Arminianism) is dependent on the response of man, they believe in conditional election. Like a Calvinist, an Arminian views election and predestination as having occurred from eternity past by means of an eternal decree. However, Arminians, unlike the Reformed (extreme and hyper-Calvinists), don't redefine foreknowledge as

149

foreordination or predestination. Their view of the free will of man does not necessitate such extreme measures.

L—Limited Atonement

The Arminians do not believe in limited atonement, that Jesus died for the elect only. They believe in unlimited atonement, that Jesus died for every human being.

I—Irresistible Grace

According to Arminianism, God's grace is resistible—not irresistible. They perceive man as possessing a free will to repent and believe while depraved, which makes man capable (according to their view) of accepting or rejecting the grace the Father offers to every human being through the death, burial, and resurrection of Christ.

P—Perseverance of the Saints

The Arminians view the believer as capable of losing his/her salvation either by committing a certain type of sin or choosing to cease believing altogether.

Keep all of this in mind as we summarize what we have discovered regarding the term *"predestined."* Remember that *"predestined"* is used only six times in the Scriptures, all in the New Testament epistles.

CHAPTER TWELVE

VI. A SUMMARY OF OUR DISCOVERIES REGARDING "PREDESTINED"

THE FOLLOWING WAS WRITTEN ASSUMING that the student might be researching only one of the six verses that address the subject of predestination. Consequently, statements included in the commentary associated with one verse may also be found in the commentary of another. Thus, a reason exists for the redundant nature of this summary. So have a wonderful time basking in the simplicity of the contextual view of "predestined." If it hasn't happened by now, it will become apparent that the opposing schools of thought are responsible for the confusion surrounding this uncomplicated, downright simple, theological matter.

We will now summarize what we have discovered regarding the term *"predestined"* by revisiting Acts 4:28, 1Corinthians 2:7, Romans 8:29, Romans 8:30, Ephesians 1:5, and Ephesians 1:11.

"Predestined" in Acts 4:28

> *to do whatever Thy hand and Thy purpose <u>predestined</u> to occur.*
> (Acts 4:28)

The Contextual View

The Father *"predestined"* the crucifixion of Christ without removing the free will of those responsible for His crucifixion.

151

The Opposing View

The opposing view perceives God as not only predestining Jesus' crucifixion, but also predestining the behavior of those responsible for Jesus' crucifixion.

How the Opposing View Came into Existence

This view results from the false idea that God must cause all things to retain His sovereignty. Extreme and hyper-Calvinism generally teach that God must cause all things to know all things, thus removing the free will of man, especially in the area of choosing Christ while depraved.

Rebuttal to the Opposing View

Had the men responsible for Jesus' death been programmed by the Father to commit these acts, having no choice in the matter, how could God remain just while punishing them for their misdeeds? Thus, Jesus' crucifixion was predestined by God while the behavior of those who nailed Him to the cross was not! Also, should God be the cause of all things, which many Calvinist believe, He must be the author of sin—an "idea" found nowhere in Scripture.

"Predestined" in 1Corinthians 2:7

> *but we speak God's wisdom in a mystery, the hidden wisdom, which*
> *God <u>predestined</u> before the ages to our glory;* (1Corinthians 2:7)

The Contextual View

God *"predestined"* that the redeemed who go on to spiritual maturity during the church age would receive *"the hidden wisdom."*

The Opposing View

The extreme and hyper-Calvinists use 1Corinthians 2:7 in an attempt to validate their view of total depravity, a total depravity which supports their view of predestination. In their opinion, *"the hidden wisdom"* of 1Corinthians 2:7 is given to the elect (as they define the elect) through spiritual regeneration. According to their ideology, God spiritually regenerates (awakens) the elect from their spiritual deadness (total depravity), and in the process, grants them the *"hidden wisdom"* of 1Corinthians 2:7. In conjunction with being spiritually regenerated and enlightened with this *"hidden wisdom,"* God bestows them the gifts of repentance and faith—which then allows them to repent, believe, and be saved/justified. (Brace yourself before reading the following sentence, for it reveals the complicated nature of this viewpoint.) Thus, according to Reformed Theology (extreme and hyper-Calvinism), repentance and faith are God's gifts that allow the elect (who, according to the Reformed view, have been predestined to salvation, from eternity past, by means of an eternal decree) to repent and believe <u>after</u> being spiritually regenerated and enlightened with the *"hidden wisdom"* of 1Corinthians 2:7. In this arrangement, spiritual regeneration <u>precedes</u> repentance and faith (believing)—a teaching found nowhere in Scripture.

How the Opposing View Came into Existence

Reformed Theology (extreme and hyper-Calvinism), in order to maintain its assessment of total depravity (that the depraved are incapable of choosing Christ), adheres to the idea that God predestined the elect to salvation, from eternity past, by my means of an eternal decree. In fact, Reformed Theology views the spiritual depravity of the lost as equivalent to a total inability to repent and believe. Hence, God (according to their perception):

(1) Was required to make the choice for the elect (through predestination and election from eternity past, by means of an eternal decree)

(2) Must spiritually regenerate the elect (and grant them the *"hidden wisdom"* of 1Corinthians 2:7) at some point after their arrival on the earth

(3) Must follow by giving them the gifts of repentance and faith so they can repent, believe, and be saved/justified

In this scenario, spiritual regeneration precedes repentance and faith, totally eliminating any need for man (in his depravity) to possess the freedom to repent and believe. This school, therefore, redefines foreknowledge as foreordination or predestination. After all, should the depraved lack the ability to repent and believe, no free decision of man (pertaining to the depraved choosing to exercise repentance and faith) would exist that God would be required to foreknow.

Rebuttal to the Opposing View

Verses such as Acts 16:31, 26:18, and Romans 10:13 confirm that faith, exercised in one's depraved state, precedes spiritual regeneration. Also, this faith is the believer's faith (Matthew 9:22, 29; Luke 7:50; 22:32; Romans 11:20)—not God's gift to those who have been predestined to salvation from eternity past (by means of an eternal decree) and spiritually regenerated at some point after their arrival on the earth, as Reformed theologians believe. Note: The fact that faith must be exercised prior to spiritual regeneration will be covered in much depth later in this *God's Heart* series.

Man's problem is not a spiritual depravity that prevents him from choosing Christ, but rather a refusal to do so. Passages such as Isaiah 7:9, Ezekiel 3:6-7, Malachi 2:2, Luke 9:5, Luke 22:67, John 4:48, Acts 3:23, Acts 22:18, Romans 1:18-20, and 2Timothy 4:3 are only a partial listing of the many verses that support this truth. Remember that depravity is covered more comprehensively in *God's Heart as it Relates to Depravity*, the third book of this *God's Heart* series.

"Predestined" in Romans 8:29

> *For whom He foreknew, He also* <u>*predestined*</u> *to become conformed to the image of His Son, that He might be the first-born among many brethren;* (Romans 8:29)

As you proceed, know that I realize the redundant nature of this section. As stated earlier, it was written so the student can quick reference any of the six verses that address predestination and gain a proper view of the passage under consideration.

The Contextual View

Predestination *("predestined")* has nothing to do with whether a person will or will not be saved. Rather, the term *"predestined"* confirms that any person who (during the church age) chooses to accept Christ (while depraved) is given a glorious future destiny in conjunction with being placed in Christ and made new. The New Testament believer's glorious future destiny is that he/she will receive a glorified *"body"* (Ephesians 1:5; Romans 8:23) at the Rapture of the church and bask in all the blessings associated with that amazing event. This glorified body will be like Jesus' resurrected body, providing enormous benefits for all church saints. Because God possesses foreknowledge, He knows beforehand who will accept Him and receive this glorious future destiny. He also knows who will not.

Be sure to make use of the diagrams included in the Reference Section.

The Opposing View

The opposing view adheres to the idea that God, by means of an eternal decree, predestined the elect (as they define the elect) to salvation from eternity past. One branch of this view, hyper-Calvinism, believes that God, from eternity past, by means of an eternal decree, predestined the elect to salvation and the non-elect to damnation. Extreme Calvinism is much the same, with God having predestined the elect to salvation, from eternity past, by means of an eternal decree, but having left the non-elect to the consequence of their sin. Remember, extreme and hyper-Calvinism are known today as Reformed Theology. Moderate Calvinists believe that God, from eternity past, and by means of an eternal decree, predestined the elect to salvation but granted man a free will to repent and believe while depraved.

Many forms of Calvinism exist. Therefore, to describe in detail what all Calvinists believe is impossible. Yet, they all view God as having predestined the elect to salvation, from eternity past, by means of an eternal decree. Arminians view God as having predestined the elect to salvation (from eternity past, by means of an eternal decree) <u>after</u> He, as a result of His foreknowledge, looked into the future and saw who would choose to repent and believe while depraved.

How the Opposing View Came into Existence

Because the extreme and hyper-Calvinists perceive the depraved as incapable of choosing Christ, God was required (according to their view) to make that choice for the elect from eternity past. The moderate Calvinists, on the other hand, view the depraved as capable of choosing Christ—but hold to the falsehood that God predestined the elect to salvation, from eternity past, by means of an eternal decree. The "elect" are individuals who have been elected and predestined to salvation, from eternity past, by means of an eternal decree, according to all forms of Calvinism). Therefore, based on each of these systems of thought, only those whom God has predestined (and elected) to salvation from eternity past (by means of an eternal decree) will be saved/justified. Rejecting the extreme views of Calvinism, the Arminians perceive God as having predestined the elect to salvation from eternity past, by means of an eternal decree) <u>after</u> He, as a result of His foreknowledge, looked into the future and saw who would choose to repent and believe while depraved (reference Diagrams 4 and 5).

155

Rebuttal to the Opposing View

The rebuttal is quite simple. New Testament believers could not have been predestined from eternity past by means of an eternal decree because foreknowledge, which is required to precede their predestination (Romans 8:29), cannot precede an eternal decree. We proved this fact when we addressed *Foreknowledge* as an independent topic, so be sure to reference those materials should you need more input. You can also review Diagrams 2 and 7 in the Reference Section. Foreknowledge can, however, precede predestination if predestination occurs in time, rather than from eternity past. Thus, predestination does not deal with who will or will not be saved, but rather with the destiny that God immediately grants to those who, during the church age, choose to repent and believe while depraved. In fact, the New Testament believer is predestined (once he/she is placed in Christ and becomes a new creation, subsequent to exercising repentance and faith while depraved) to receive a glorified body at the Rapture of the church (read Ephesians 1:5 with Romans 8:23).

The hyper-Calvinists, extreme Calvinists, moderate Calvinists, and Arminians fail to differentiate between the blessings associated with salvation and salvation itself. In other words, instead of viewing predestination as relating to the glorious future destiny that New Testament believers receive once they are placed in Christ (after choosing to repent and believe while depraved), they perceive God as having predestined the elect to salvation from eternity past by means of an eternal decree. This error has generated numerous contradictions which are impossible to reconcile—that is, when exposed to the full counsel of God's Word.

"Predestined" in Romans 8:30

> *and whom He <u>predestined</u>, these He also called; and whom He called, these He also justified; and whom He justified, these He also glorified.* (Romans 8:30)

The Contextual View

Once a person, during the church age, exercises personal repentance and faith while depraved, the Holy Spirit places that individual into Christ (1Corinthians 12:13). Only then is he/she made *"new"* (2Corinthians 5:17) and *"predestined"* (Romans 8:30) to receive a glorified *"body"* (Ephesians 1:5; Romans 8:23)—along with all the benefits that accompany that magnificent experience. Each church saint will receive his/her glorified body at the Rapture of the church. Romans 8:3

does <u>not</u> describe the chronological order of events in the New Testament believer's salvation experience.

The Opposing View

Some individuals have concluded that Romans 8:29-30 describes the chronological order of events in the believer's salvation experience. Consequently, they suppose that God: (1) foreknew the elect (actually foreordained or predestined the elect, as they define the term "elect," to salvation, from eternity past, by means of an eternal decree—Romans 8:29 and 30) (2) calls the elect to salvation sometime after they are born physically (Romans 8:30) (3) justifies, or saves, the elect (Romans 8:30) (4) glorifies the elect after physical death (Romans 8:30).

How the Opposing View Came into Existence

This view, in most cases, results from an improper understanding of depravity, which, according to Reformed Theology (extreme and hyper-Calvinism), does not allow the depraved to choose Christ. Consequently, God (in their minds) made that decision for the elect from eternity past, by means of an eternal decree, by predestining and electing them to salvation. Even moderate Calvinism and Arminianism, although granting man a free will to repent and believe while depraved, view God as having predestined the elect to salvation from eternity past by means of an eternal decree. Both of these arrangements are totally unworkable and, therefore, extremely contradictory. Their error is incorrectly assuming that believers (the elect) were predestined and elected to salvation from eternity past rather than predestined to blessings associated with salvation in conjunction with being made new. (Review Diagrams 2 and 7 in the Reference Section.)

Rebuttal to the Opposing View

All forms of Calvinism and Arminianism err due to one common misconception. They view predestination as having to do with a person's future destiny (in hell or heaven) rather than blessings associated with salvation, blessings that are guaranteed once the depraved

Calvinism and Arminianism err due to one common misconception.

157

(during the church age) exercise personal repentance and faith and are predestined in association with being made *"new"* (2Corinthians 5:17).

New Testament believers could not have been predestined from eternity past by means of an eternal decree because foreknowledge, which is required to precede predestination (Romans 8:29), cannot precede an eternal decree. We proved this fact when we addressed *Foreknowledge* as an independent topic, so those materials can be reviewed along with Diagram 2 in the Reference Section. Foreknowledge can, however, precede predestination if predestination occurs in time rather than from eternity past (reference Diagram 7). Therefore, the New Testament believer is predestined (once he/she is placed in Christ and becomes new—subsequent to exercising repentance and faith while depraved) to receive a glorified body at the Rapture of the church (read Ephesians 1:5 with Romans 8:23). Can we even begin to imagine the positive ramifications of this wonderful occasion? Thus, to perceive God as having predestined individuals to salvation from eternity past is doctrinally unsound.

We must make sure to view the word *"glorified"* (Romans 8:30) in its context. It does not point to the future glorified body that the New Testament believer is *"predestined"* (in time, rather than from eternity past) to receive at the Rapture of the church (Ephesians 1:5; Romans 8:23). *"Glorified"* describes the state of the soul and spirit of the New Testament believer the moment he/she is placed in Christ and made *"new"* (2Corinthians 5:17)—subsequent to repenting and believing while depraved. Why is this the case? The words *"foreknew," "predestined," "called," "justified,"* and *"glorified"* are all in the aorist tense and, thus, pertain to things that have already occurred in the New Testament believer's experience. Hence, a believer today has already been foreknown, *"predestined," "called," "justified,"* and *"glorified."* Since *"glorified"* is in the same, aorist tense as *"foreknew," "predestined," "called,"* and *"justified,"* the souls and spirits of all believers during the church age are *"glorified"* in conjunction with becoming new creations in Christ. Yet, church saints will not receive their glorified bodies, to which they were predestined when placed in Christ, subsequent to repenting and believing while depraved, until the Rapture of the church (Ephesians 1:5; Romans 8:23).

The hyper-Calvinists, extreme Calvinists, moderate Calvinists, and Arminians reap severe theological ramifications for failing to differentiate between the blessings associated with salvation and salvation itself. Instead of viewing predestination in relation to the glorious future destiny New Testament believers receive once they are placed in Christ (after choosing to repent and believe while depraved), they perceive God as having predestined to salvation from eternity past by means of an eternal decree, those who will be saved. This erroneous belief has generated numerous contradictions which are impossible to reconcile, such as the contradiction recorded next.

Arminianism and all forms of Calvinism perceive Romans 8:30 as teaching that believers were predestined and elected to salvation before they are born (from eternity past, by means of an eternal decree). Such a view, however, would allow Romans 8:30 to teach that the *"predestined"* of Arminianism and Calvinism who are not yet in existence are presently *"called," "justified,"* and *"glorified"*—since *"predestined," "called," "justified,"* and *"glorified"* are all in the past tense. Stated differently, had future believers been *"predestined"* to salvation from eternity past, they would presently be *"called," "justified,"* and *"glorified."* This arrangement, however, would cause them to be *"justified"* and *"glorified"* prior to existing as well as *"justified"* and *"glorified"* at physical birth. Therefore, passages such as Ephesians 2:3 discredit both Arminianism and all forms of Calvinism (including Reformed Theology), for all persons arrive on the earth *"children of wrath."*

"Predestined" in Ephesians 1:5

> He <u>predestined</u> us to adoption as sons through Jesus Christ to Himself, according to the kind intention of His will, (Ephesians 1:5)

The Contextual View

God (in time, rather than from eternity past by means of an eternal decree) predestines all New Testament believers *"to adoption as sons"* in conjunction with making them new—after they, in their depravity, exercise personal repentance and faith. Thus, God predestined us in conjunction with placing us in Christ and making us new. According to Romans 8:23, the *"adoption as sons"* is *"the redemption of the body."* Thus, the New Testament believer, once he/she exercises repentance and faith (while depraved) and becomes a new creation (through being placed in Christ), is *"predestined"* to one day receive a glorified body. This body will be received at the Rapture of the church.

The Opposing View

The opposing view considers Ephesians 1:5 to be teaching that God predestined the elect (as they define the "elect") to salvation, from eternity past, by means of an eternal decree. They support this belief by equating *"adoption as sons"* with salvation from sins.

How the Opposing View Came into Existence

God was required, according to this mindset, to predestine the elect (as they define the "elect") to salvation, from eternity past, by means of an eternal decree. Within Reformed Theology (extreme and hyper-Calvinism), this option is the only one available due to their viewing the depraved as incapable of choosing to repent and believe. Moderate Calvinism and Arminianism hold to the same basic view of predestination as Reformed Theology (that it is to salvation rather than to blessings associated with salvation), yet grant man the freedom to repent and believe while depraved. Thus, an incorrect perception of predestination results from their viewing New Testament believers as having been predestined to salvation from eternity past rather than predestined to blessings associated with salvation in conjunction with being made new.

Rebuttal to the Opposing View

Predestination could not have occurred from eternity past, by means of an eternal decree, because foreknowledge is required precede it (Romans 8:29). Nothing can precede an eternal decree (Reference Diagrams 2 and 7.) Also, unregenerate man is <u>not</u> so spiritually depraved that he cannot make a choice to repent and believe—a matter discussed in much detail in *God's Heart as it Relates to Depravity*, the third book of this *God's Heart* series.

"Predestined" in Ephesians 1:11

> *also we have obtained an inheritance, having been <u>predestined</u> according to His purpose who works all things after the counsel of his will,* (Ephesians 1:11)

The Contextual View

During the church age, God predestines all believers to blessings in conjunction with placing them in Christ (subsequent to their exercising personal repentance and faith while depraved). New Testament believers, therefore, are predestined in time rather than from eternity past. Thus, church saints are predestined, once they are placed in Christ and made new, to receive glorified bodies at the Rapture of the church (confirmed by Ephesians 1:5 and Romans 8:23). Many blessings will accompany this magnificent event.

160

The Opposing View

As was the case with Romans 8:29, Romans 8:30, and Ephesians 1:5, the opposing view (adopted by extreme and hyper-Calvinism, moderate Calvinism, and Arminianism) depicts God as having predestined the elect (as they would define the elect) to salvation, from eternity past, by means of an eternal decree. Consequently, they perceive the elect as having been predestined to salvation from eternity past.

How the Opposing View Came into Existence

Reformed Theology's view of predestination (Reformed Theology being extreme and hyper-Calvinism) stems from an improper perception of depravity—which presupposes that the depraved (the spiritually unregenerated) are incapable of choosing Christ. Moderate Calvinism and Arminianism hold to the same basic view of predestination as Reformed Theology (that it is to salvation rather than to blessings associated with salvation), yet grant man the freedom to repent and believe while depraved. Thus, each of these systems of thought portray God as having predestined "the elect" to salvation, from eternity past, by means of an eternal decree.

Rebuttal to the Opposing View

According to Romans 8:29, foreknowledge, meaning "to know beforehand," must precede the predestination of a New Testament believer. However, should predestination be by means of an eternal decree (as Calvinism and Arminianism suppose), room for foreknowledge to precede predestination would not exist (refer to Diagrams 2 and 7). For God to have predestined believers to salvation by means of an eternal decree is, therefore, impossible. These facts refute all forms of Calvinism (including Reformed Theology) and Arminianism.

Also, note the phrase, *"predestined according to His purpose"* (Ephesians 1:11). We learned earlier that the action or entity that follows the words *"according to"* (such as God's *"purpose"* in Ephesians 1:11) must occur (or exist) <u>before</u> the action or entity that precedes the words *"according to"* (such as *"predestined"* in Ephesians 1:11). Thus:

If **A** is <u>according to</u> **B**

Then **B** <u>precedes</u> **A**

Ephesians 1:11 proves, therefore, that God's *"purpose"* must precede the predestination of a New Testament believer. Because God's purposes are *"eternal"* (Ephesians 3:11), predestination could not have occurred from eternity past, by means of an eternal decree, due to the requirement that His *"purpose"* (Ephesians 1:11) must precede it. Nothing can precede that which is eternal. Thus, had we been predestined from eternity past by means of an eternal decree, no room would exist for God's eternal purpose to have preceded our predestination. Hence, to perceive the predestination of New Testament believers as occurring in time and in association with their becoming new creations in Christ is the proper view. This sequence leaves ample room for God's foreknowledge (Romans 8:29) to precede the New Testament believer's predestination, as evidenced by Diagrams 2, 7, and 8 in the Reference Section. This arrangement also allows God's *"purpose"* (Ephesians 1:11), which is *"eternal"* (Ephesians 3:11), to precede the New Testament believer's predestination—as required by Ephesians 1:11.

Final Words

This concludes our study of the term *"predestined."* Our discoveries will serve us well as we consider our next topics of interest, *Sovereignty/Free Will.* The journey that lies ahead should be exciting as well as encouraging. Why wouldn't it be if the end result is a proper view of the heart of our, sovereign, all knowing, all powerful, gracious, forgiving, and loving God. Jehovah will honor the investment you are making in His Word:

> *All Scripture is inspired by God and profitable for teaching, for reproof, for correction, for training in righteousness; that the man of God may be adequate, equipped for every good work.* (2Timothy 3:16-17)

Foreknowledge Predestination Scripture Index

Scripture — page number

Diagram 1

Eternity
No Beginning And No End

Diagram 2

Why God's Foreknowledge Cannot
Precede His Eternal Decrees

Calvinism and Arminianism adhere to the idea that the elect were elected (chosen) and predestined to salvation from eternity past by means of an eternal decree. This arrangement is impossible, and the following explains why.

Scripture teaches that God's decrees are eternal (Jeremiah 5:22), having always existed in His heart.

> *'Do you not fear Me?' declares the LORD. 'Do you not tremble in My presence? For I have placed the sand as a boundary for the sea, An eternal decree, so it cannot cross over it. Though the waves toss, yet they cannot prevail; Though they roar, yet they cannot cross over it.* (Jeremiah 5:22)

Scripture also requires God's foreknowledge (which means to know beforehand) to precede the predestination and election (choosing) of a New Testament believer.

> *For those whom He foreknew, He also predestined to become conformed to the image of His Son, so that He would be the firstborn among many brethren;* (Romans 8:29)

> *Peter, an apostle of Jesus Christ, To those who reside as aliens, scattered throughout Pontus, Galatia, Cappadocia, Asia, and Bithynia, who are chosen according to the foreknowledge of God the Father, by the sanctifying work of the Spirit, to obey Jesus Christ and be sprinkled with His blood : May grace and peace be yours in the fullest measure.* (1Peter 1:1-2)

Should God's foreknowledge, meaning "to know beforehand," precede His eternal decrees, eternity would have a beginning (a starting point)—a total impossibility.

Because God's decrees are eternal (Jeremiah 5:22), and foreknowledge is required to precede the predestination and election (choosing) of the New Testament believer (Romans 8:29; 1Peter 1:1-2), for God to have predestined or elected (chosen) New Testament believers to salvation from eternity past by means of an eternal decree is impossible.

The Scriptures teach that New Testament believers are elected and predestined to blessings (rather than to salvation), a predestination and election that occur when they are placed in Christ subsequent to their exercising personal repentance and faith while depraved. This truth allows God's foreknowledge to precede the predestination and election of a New Testament believer, as displayed below.

FOREKNOWLEDGE	Predestination of New Testament Believers when they are spiritually regenerated (saved). Election/Chosenness of New Testament Believers when they are spiritually regenerated (saved).

∞

167

Diagram 3

God, The Eternal I AM

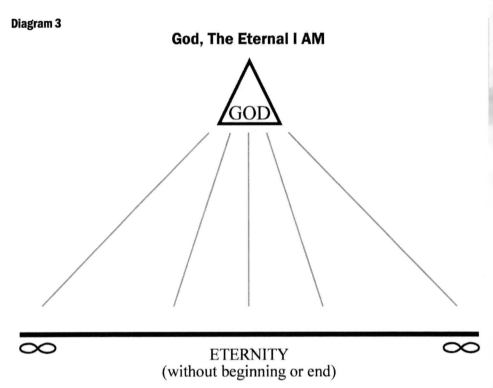

ETERNITY
(without beginning or end)

God sees all events, from eternity past through eternity future, throughout His eternal existence. In other words, He possesses the ability to see all things at once. He therefore, is never caught off guard since He possesses knowledge of all past, present, and future events. God is not required to cause events to foreknow them.

Diagram 4

Arminius' Beliefs

Election
Predestination

| FOREKNOWLEDGE |

Arminius' belief regarding foreknowledge affected his view of salvation. He believed that God looked into the future and, by means of His eternal foreknowledge, saw who would choose to repent and believe while depraved. God then, based on Arminius' theology, elected (chose) and predestined these future believers to salvation from eternity past by means of an eternal decree.

Diagram 5

What Arminius' Belief System Actually Communicates

Election
Predestination
God's Foreknowledge

Arminius believed that God's decrees, as well as His foreknowledge, are eternal. He also believed that certain individuals were elected (chosen) and predestined to salvation by means of an eternal decree. This order, however, leaves no room for God's foreknowledge to precede the New Testament believer's election and predestination. Arminius' theological chronology actually stacked election, predestination, and God's foreknowledge on top of each other, when Romans 8:29 and 1Peter 1:1-2 require God's foreknowledge to precede the election and predestination of a New Testament believer. Arminius arrived at this contradiction due to equating the blessings associated with salvation with salvation itself.

Diagram 6

Calvin's Beliefs

Election
Predestination
(God's Foreknowledge = Foreordination or Predestination)

Calvin believed that God, from eternity past and by means of an eternal decree, elected (chose) and predestined the elect to salvation. This view contradicts Romans 8:29 and 1Peter 1:1-2, both of which require God's foreknowledge to precede the election (chosenness) and predestination of a New Testament believer. Thus, Calvin's theology fails to provide room for foreknowledge to precede the election (chosenness) and predestination of a New Testament believer. Therefore, Calvin deemed foreknowledge as synonymous with foreordination or predestination. In other words Calvin redefined foreknowledge as foreordination or predestination, which required the writing of volumes of materials in an effort to remedy such contradiction. Calvin arrived at this error due to equating the blessings associated with salvation with salvation itself.

Diagram 7

The Remedy to Calvin's and Arminius' Error

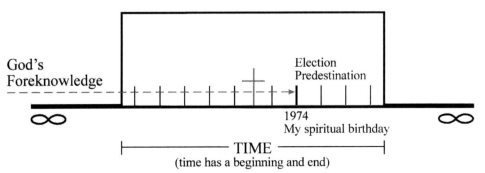

The remedy to Calvin's and Arminius' error is found in allowing God's foreknowledge in this case to point to His foreknowledge of the thoughts, actions, and decisions of those who choose to repent and believe during the church age. Once they exercise repentance and faith while depraved, they are placed in Christ. God then predestines them to one day receive a glorified body (Romans 8:23; Ephesians 1:5). He also elects (chooses) them in Christ (Ephesians 1:4), after they repent and believe while depraved, bestowing upon them the office (gifting--1Peter 4:10) to which he elects them.

New Testament believers are placed in Christ, subsequent to repenting and believing while depraved, and only then are elected (chosen) and predestined. At that point they receive eternal life, life with no beginning and no end, and are viewed by the Father as having always been in Christ (Ephesians 1:4).

Diagram 8

Scriptural Election/Chosenness and Predestination

The Father sees all New Testament believers, subsequent to their exercising personal repentance and faith while depraved and being made new, as having always been in Christ due to the type of life they receive at the point of salvation - eternal life.

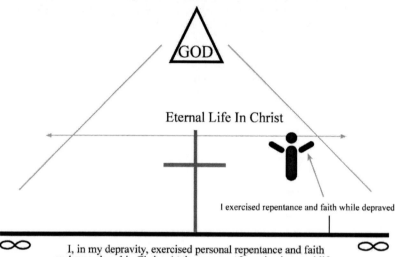

The Holy Spirit places those seeking salvation during the church age into Christ when they repent and exercise faith while depraved (1Corinthians 12:13). Once this occurs, God makes them new (2Corinthians 5:17). He also predestines them (at that time) to receive glorified bodies at the Rapture of the church (Ephesians 1:5; Romans 8:23; 1Corinthians 15:35-58; 1Thessalonians 4:13-18). They are also elected/chosen (at that time) to office due to having been placed into Christ, the Father's elect/chosen one (Luke 9:35; Isaiah 42:1), Who was elected/chosen to the office of Messiah. The office to which New Testament believers are elected/chosen is the special office or position (gift) they receive (1Peter 4:10) in conjunction with being placed in Christ and made new. Therefore, New Testament believers were not predestined and elected/chosen to salvation from eternity past by means of an eternal decree. They are predestined the moment they are made new in Christ subsequent to repenting and believing while depraved; predestined to receive a new body (Ephesians 1:5; Romans 8:23) at the Rapture of the church. They are also elected/chosen to office when placed in Christ, subsequent to repenting and believing while depraved, Christ having been elected/chosen to office, the office of Messiah. Ephesians 1:4 states:

> *just as He chose us in Him before the foundation of the world, that we should be holy and blameless before Him. (Ephesians 1:4)*

Once New Testament believers are placed in Christ, they receive His kind of life, eternal life (Romans 6:23; Colossians 3:4), life with no beginning and no end. As a result, the Father sees them as having always been in Christ, even *"before the foundation of the world"* (Ephesians 1:4). Consequently, their point of entry into Christ is when they repent and believe while depraved; but once they are placed in Him through the power of the Holy Spirit (1Corinthians 12:13), the Father sees them as having always been in His holy Son. He will continue to view New Testament believers in this manner throughout eternity.

Diagram 9

The Predestination of Jesus' Death and the Hidden Wisdom

Acts 4:27-28; 1Corinthians 2:7

For trully in this city there were gathered together against Your holy servant Jesus, whom You annointed, both Herod and Pontius Pilate, along with the Gentiles and the peoples of Israel, to do whatever Your hand and Your purpose predestined to occur. (Acts 4:27-28)

but we speak God's wisdom in a mystery, the hidden wisdom which God predestined before the ages to our glory; (1Corinthians 2:7)

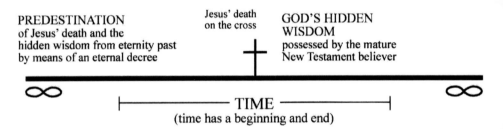

PREDESTINATION
of Jesus' death and the
hidden wisdom from eternity past
by means of an eternal decree

Jesus' death
on the cross

GOD'S HIDDEN
WISDOM
possessed by the mature
New Testament believer

∞   ——————— TIME ———————   ∞
(time has a beginning and end)

The Scriptures do not require that the predestination of the cross (Acts 4:27-28) and the hidden wisdom of God (1Corinthians 2:7) be preceded by God's foreknowledge. This difference leaves room for God to have predestined the cross and the hidden wisdom from eternity past by means of an eternal decree. Such an arrangement is unlike the predestination of the New Testament believer, which occurs in time, and requires God's foreknowledge to precede it.

172

Diagram 10

Reformed Theology (Extreme and Hyper-Calvinism)

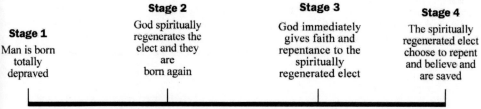

Stage 1
Man is born totally depraved

Stage 2
God spiritually regenerates the elect and they are born again

Stage 3
God immediately gives faith and repentance to the spiritually regenerated elect

Stage 4
The spiritually regenerated elect choose to repent and believe and are saved

This view is contradictory because Scripture equates spiritual regeneration and being born again with salvation. With Reformed Theology's configuration, believers would be saved twice--a total impossibility.

The Scriptual View

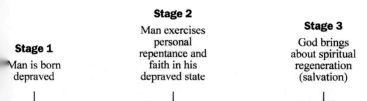

Stage 1
Man is born depraved

Stage 2
Man exercises personal repentance and faith in his depraved state

Stage 3
God brings about spiritual regeneration (salvation)

Be aware that man is brought out of his state of depravity and into the kingdom in a flash, in fact, less than a flash. Therefore, the brevity of time between man's choice to repent and believe while depraved and God's act of spiritual regeneration (salvation) is impossible to imagine.

Diagram 11

Hyper-Calvinism (One Brand of Reformed Theology)

| Predestination unconditional election: the elect to salvation the non-elect to damnation | God spiritually regenerates the depraved elect | God bestows the gifts of repentance and faith to the spiritually regenerated elect | The spiritually regenerated elect repent, believe, and are saved |

∞ *From eternity past by means of an eternal decree*

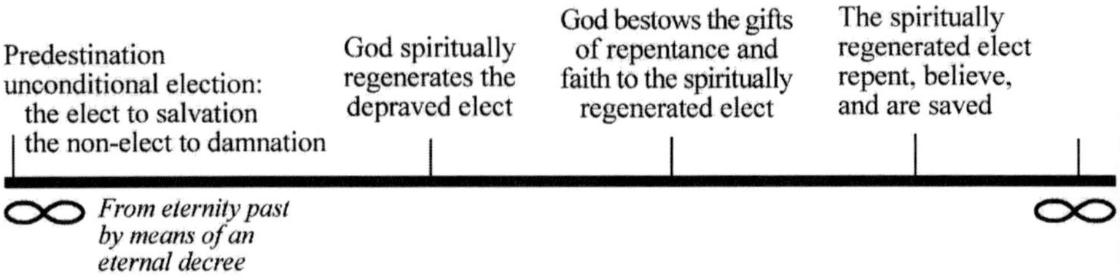

Strong (Extreme) Calvinism (A Second Brand of Reformed Theology)

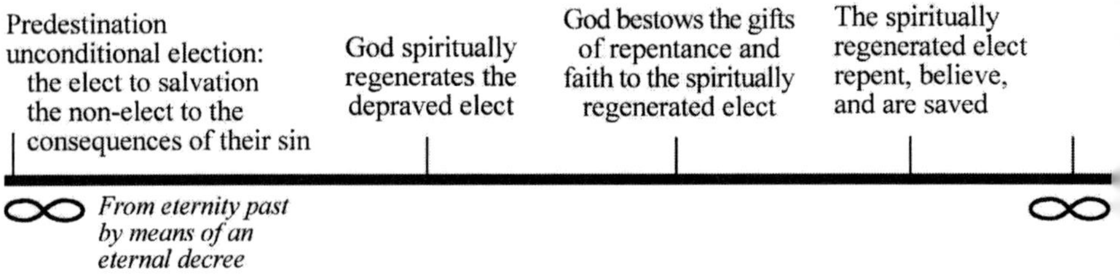

| Predestination unconditional election: the elect to salvation the non-elect to the consequences of their sin | God spiritually regenerates the depraved elect | God bestows the gifts of repentance and faith to the spiritually regenerated elect | The spiritually regenerated elect repent, believe, and are saved |

∞ *From eternity past by means of an eternal decree*

Moderate Calvinism

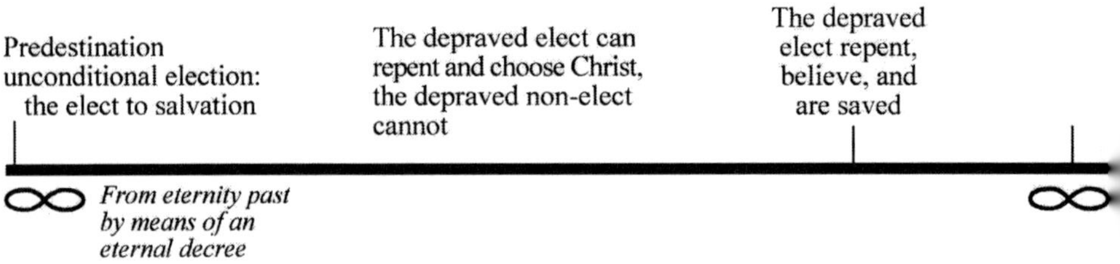

| Predestination unconditional election: the elect to salvation | The depraved elect can repent and choose Christ, the depraved non-elect cannot | The depraved elect repent, believe, and are saved |

∞ *From eternity past by means of an eternal decree*

Arminianism

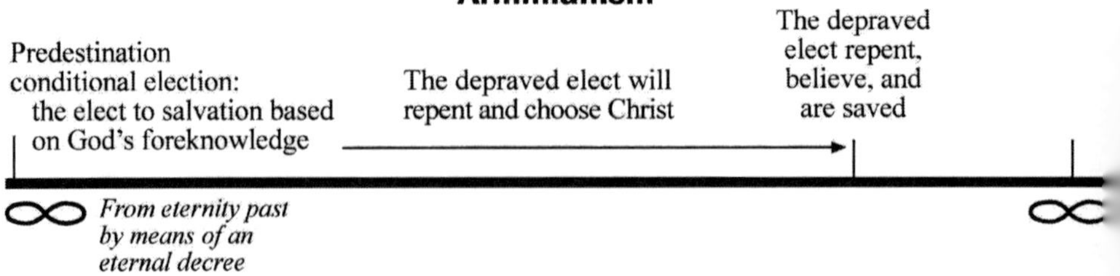

| Predestination conditional election: the elect to salvation based on God's foreknowledge | The depraved elect will repent and choose Christ | The depraved elect repent, believe, and are saved |

∞ *From eternity past by means of an eternal decree*

174

Diagram 12

Hyper Supralapsarianism	Strong (Extreme) Infralapsarianism	Moderate Sublapsarianism	Arminian Wesleyanism
(1) Decree to elect some and reprobate others	(1) Decree to create all	(1) Decree to create all	(1) Decree to create all
(2) Decree to create both the elect and the non-elect	(2) Decree to permit the Fall	(2) Decree to permit the Fall	(2) Decree to permit the Fall
(3) Decree to permit the Fall	(3) Decree to elect some and pass others by	(3) Decree to provide salvation for all	(3) Decree to provide salvation for all
(4) Decree to provide salvation only for the elect	(4) Decree to provide salvation only for the elect	(4) Decree to elect those who believe and pass by those who do not	(4) Decree to elect based on the foreseen faith of believers
(5) Decree to apply salvation only to the elect	(5) Decree to apply salvation only to the elect	(5) Decree to apply salvation only to believers (who cannot lose it)	(5) Decree to apply salvation only to believers (who can lose it)

Bibliography

[1] Dave Hunt, *What Love Is This?*, Third Edition, Published by The Berean Call, 2006, page 283, Used by permission.

[2] Ibid., pages 287.

[3] John Calvin, *Institutes of the Christian Religion,* Book 3; Chapter 21; Section 5.

[4] Ibid., Book 3; Chapter 21; Section 7.

[5] Dave Hunt, *What Love Is This?*, Third Edition, Published by The Berean Call, 2006, page 286, Used by permission.

[6] Ibid., page 183.

[7] Hugh Ross, *The Creator and the Cosmos; how the greatest discoveries of the century reveal God,* Published by Reasons To Believe, 1993, 1995, 2001, NavPress, pages 73-74, Used by permission.

[8] Roger T. Forster and V. Paul Marston, *GOD'S Strategy in Human History*, Published by Send The Light Trust, 1973, page 191, Used by permission.

[9] Justin Martyr, *The First Apology of Justin,* Chapter 28.

[10] Ibid., Chapter 44.

[11] Ibid., Chapter 45.

[12] Justin Martyr, *Dialogue with Trypho,* Chapter 141.

[13] Origen, Against Celsus: Book II; Chapter 20

[14] Roger T. Forster and V. Paul Marston, *GOD'S Strategy in Human History*, Published by Send The Light Trust, 1973, page 192, Used by permission.

[15] John Calvin, *Institutes of the Christian Religion,* Book 3; Chapter 23; Section 6.

[16] R.C. Sproul Jr., *Almighty Over All: Understanding the Sovereignty of God,* pages 52-54, Published by Baker Books, a division of Baker Publishing Group, Copyright 1999, Used by permission.

[17] Reprinted by permission. *The Love of God: He Will Do Whatever It Takes to Make Us Holy,* John MacArthur Jr, © 1998, page 17, Thomas Nelson Inc. Nashville, Tennessee. All rights reserved.

[18] John Calvin, *Institutes of the Christian Religion,* Book 3; Chapter 21; Section 5.

[19] Ibid., Book 3; Chapter 21; Section 7.

[20] Ibid., Book 3; Chapter 24; Section 17.

[21] Jacobus Arminius, *The Works of James Arminius;* Volume 1; Translated from the Latin by James Nichols; *On Predestination; My Own Sentiments on Predestination*

[22] John Piper and Pastoral Staff, *"TULIP: What We Believe about the Five Points of Calvinism: Position Paper of the Pastoral Staff"*, Minneapolis, MN: Desiring God Foundation, 1997, 22, Used by permission.

[23] Wayne Grudem, *Bible Doctrine, Essential Teachings of the Christian Faith,* Published by Zondervan, 1999, page 286, Used by permission.

[24] Roger T. Forster and V. Paul Marston, *GOD'S Strategy in Human History*, Published by Send The Light Trust, 1973, page 189, Used by permission.

[25] Dave Hunt, *What Love Is This?*, Third Edition, Published by The Berean Call, 2006, page 281, Used by permission.

[26] John F. MacArthur, *The MacArthur New Testament Commentary, Ephesians*, Published by Moody Bible Institute of Chicago, 1986, page 14, Used by permission.

[27] John Calvin, *Institutes of the Christian Religion*, Book 3; Chapter 22; Section 1.

[28] Ibid., Book 3; Chapter 22; Section 1.

[29] Ibid.

[30] Copyright 1995, 2011 John MacArthur Jr., *Saved Without A Doubt*, Third Edition, page 59, Published by David C Cook. Publisher permission required to produce. All rights reserved.

[31] Dave Hunt, *What Love Is This?*, Third Edition, Published by The Berean Call, 2006, page 280, Used by permission.

[32] John Piper and Pastoral Staff, *"TULIP: What We Believe about the Five Points of Calvinism: Position Paper of the Pastoral Staff"*, Minneapolis, MN: Desiring God Foundation, 1997, 22, Used by permission.

[33] Dave Hunt, *What Love Is This?*, Third Edition, Published by The Berean Call, 2006, page 299, Used by permission.

[34] Norman L. Geisler, *Systematic Theology, Volume Three, Sin, Salvation*, page 381, Published by Bethany House, a division of Baker Publishing Group, Copyright 2004, Used by permission.

[35] John Calvin, *Institutes of the Christian Religion*, Book 3; Chapter 21; Section 7.

[36] Dave Hunt, *What Love Is This?*, Third Edition, Published by The Berean Call, 2006, page 119, Used by permission.

[37] Ibid., page 282.

[38] Ibid., page 172.

[39] John Piper, *The Justification of God*, Second Edition, page 49, Published by Baker Books, a division of Baker Publishing Group, Copyright 1993, Used by permission.

[40] Reprinted by permission. *The MacArthur Study Bible*, John MacArthur, © 2006, Thomas Nelson Inc. Nashville, Tennessee. All rights reserved. Commentary on Romans 9:11, page 1710.

[41] Wayne Grudem, *Bible Doctrine, Essential Teachings of the Christian Faith*, Published by Zondervan, 1999, page 287, Used by permission.

[42] Edwin H. Palmer, *The Five Points of Calvinism*, Twentieth Printing, pages 85-87, Published by Bethany House, a division of Baker Publishing Group, Copyright 1999, Used by permission.

[43] John Calvin, *Institutes of the Christian Religion*, Book 3; Chapter 21; Section 1.

[44] Ibid., Book 3; Chapter 23; Section 7.

[45] Edwin H. Palmer, *The Five Points of Calvinism*, Twentieth Printing, pages 24-25, Published by Bethany House, a division of Baker Publishing Group, Copyright 1999, Used by permission.

[46] Taken from *Chosen by God*, by R.C. Sproul, pages 36-37, © 1986 by Tyndale House Publishers, Used by permission of Tyndale House Publishers, Inc. All rights reserved.

[47] Ibid.

[48] Ibid.

[49] John Calvin, *Institutes of the Christian Religion*, Book 3; Chapter 21; Section 2.

[50] Ibid., Book 3, Chapter 23; Section 2.

[51] John F. MacArthur, *The MacArthur New Testament Commentary, Ephesians*, Published by Moody Bible Institute of Chicago, 1986, page 11, Used by permission.

[52] Taken from *Chosen by God,* by R.C. Sproul, page 15, © 1986 by Tyndale House Publishers, Used by permission of Tyndale House Publishers, Inc. All rights reserved.

[53] Aurelius Augustine, *On the Soul and its Origin*, Originally Written A.D. 419, Book 4; Chapter 16.

[54] John Calvin, *Treatises on the Eternal Predestination of God,* Translated by Henry Cole: 38 Calvin's Calvinism.

[55] John Calvin, *Institutes of the Christian Religion,* Book 3; Chapter 21; Section 1.

[56] Ibid., Book 3; Chapter 21; Section 4.

[57] Ibid., Book 3; Chapter 23; Section 1.

[58] Ibid., Book 3; Chapter 23; Section 3.

[59] Ibid., Book 3; Chapter 23; Section 6.

[60] Ibid., Book 3; Chapter 23; Section 10.

[61] Ibid., Book 3; Chapter 21; Section 7.

[62] Ibid., Book 1; Chapter 15; Section 8.

[63] Ibid., Book 3; Chapter 23; Section 7.

[64] Ibid., Book 3; Chapter 23; Section 8.

[65] Ibid., Book 3; Chapter 21; Section 2.

[66] Ibid., Book 3; Chapter 21; Section 3.

[67] Ibid., Book 3; Chapter 23; Section 9.

[68] Ibid., Book 3; Chapter 23; Section 2.

[69] Laurence M. Vance, *The Other Side of Calvinism*, Published by Vance Publications, 1999, page 236, Used by permission.

[70] Dave Hunt, *What Love Is This?*, Third Edition, Published by The Berean Call, 2006, page 426, Used by permission.

[71] The Canons of Dordt, The Decision of the Synod of Dordt on the Five Main Points of Doctrine in Dispute in the Netherlands, *Devine Election and Reprobation, The Judgment Concerning Devine Predestination*, 1618-1619, Article VI.

[72] Dave Hunt, *What Love Is This?*, Third Edition, Published by The Berean Call, 2006, page 244, Used by permission.

[73] Ibid., page 166.

[74] www.christianhistorymagazine.org, Issue 15, Pope John Paul II on Augustine, 1987. Copyright © 1987 Christians History Magazine, Used by permission.

[75] Timothy George, *Theology of the Reformers*, Published by Broadman Press, 1988, page 68, Used by permission.

[76] Norman L. Geisler, *Chosen But Free*, Second Edition, page 120, Published by Bethany House, a division of Baker Publishing Group, Copyright 2001, Used by permission.

[77] Ibid., page 121.

[78] Ibid.

[79] Ibid.

CPSIA information can be obtained at www.ICGtesting.com
Printed in the USA
LVOW13s1814180214

374243LV00002B/3/P

9 781627 270205